THE SUPERNATURAL AND PREACHING

or

THE

MISSOURI CHRISTIAN LECTURES,

DELIVERED AT

INDEPENDENCE, MO.,

JULY, 1883.

---

*PUBLISHED FOR THE
MISSOURI CHRISTIAN LECTURESHIP.*

Old Paths Book Club
BOX V • 8877 MISSION DRIVE
ROSEMEAD, CALIFORNIA
1955

Copyrighted, 1883,
by JOHN BURNS.

PHOTOLITHOPRINTED BY CUSHING - MALLOY, INC.
ANN ARBOR, MICHIGAN, UNITED STATES OF AMERICA
1955

"Before the close of the present century, the supreme questions before men for their final decision will be the religious questions."
—GUIZOT.

CONTENTS.

I. INTRODUCTION — By Isaac Errett . . 5
II. ADDRESS OF WELCOME — By Prof. E. A. Higgason 7

LECTURES.

I. THE TWO REVELATIONS — By A. B. Jones 9
II. THE ORIGIN AND GROWTH OF FREE THOUGHT — By J. W. Monser 34
III. VALUE OF METAPHYSICAL STUDY AND ITS RELATION TO RELIGIOUS THOUGHT — By Prof. O. C. Hill 58
IV. PREACHERS' METHODS — By Prof. J. W. McGarvey 83
V. INSPIRATION — By Isaac Errett . . . 108

INTRODUCTION.

THE following pages contain essays and discussions relating to questions which, at present, occupy a prominent place in the public mind. The Missouri Christian Lectureship was instituted for the study and discussion of such questions — not because Christian fellowship depends on an agreement touching any questions of a scientific or speculative character, but because, in the advocacy and defense of the Christian faith, it is needful to understand all the current discussions that threaten that faith, and desirable that the preachers of the gospel should be as nearly agreed as possible in their views of such questions and in their methods of dealing with them. United simply on one faith in the Lord Jesus Christ and obedience to him — having no human creed to dictate to us what views we shall hold on the great variety of theological, scientific and philosophical questions that are thrust upon public attention, our way to a common understanding and to unity of sentiments, so far as such questions are concerned, is that of *free discussion*, in which all may, without fear of incurring the *odium theologieum*, speak out freely what is in him, to be subjected in brotherly love, to the criticism of his brethren. Thus may we prove all things, and hold fast that which is good. By this means, and not by blind or tame submission to a human creed, we hope to reach a general agreement, even on questions in reference to which unity of sentiment, if not essential, is still desirable.

Moreover, we have many young ministers whose reading is limited, and whose convictions on many questions which they need to understand in order to an enlightened advocacy of the gospel, are necessarily unripe. Among our older ministers, some are well read on one question, some on another. Tastes, habits, opportunities differ. Hence, in this Lectureship, we form a common stock, each contributing what is in his possession for the common good, and all becoming enriched by others, while giving of their own for the general welfare. We thus seek to become better acquainted with the living issues of the times, and learn how to deal with them. It is vain to ignore the questions which have taken possession of the public mind, and worse than vain to attempt to dispose of them without an honest acquaintance with them. In these mutual communications and free interchange of thought, we may help each other to a better understanding of many important subjects, concerning which the heavy exactions on time and strength in ministerial service forbid to many the thoroughness of study which is desirable.

Two things must be constantly kept in mind: —

1. The common ground — that of the faith in Jesus and obedience to Him, — is to be held sacred, and must not come into dispute.

2. Outside of this, while recognizing the right of freedom of opinion and of discussion, it must be constantly seen to that this liberty runs not into licentiousness, and that profitless questions are carefully avoided.

Within these limits, it is hoped these investigations will contribute to a unanimity of sentiment and uniformity of practice which no creed authority can create or enforce.

There is a bold and daring materialistic theory now afloat — sublime in its boldness and comprehensiveness — which not only seeks to account for the phenomena of the physical universe, but pushes its researches, and plants its godless philosophy into the realms of morals and religion as well, attempting to subject the whole material and spiritual universe to the dominion of blind mechanical force, and to swamp the soul in the darkness and despair of Agnosticism. It strikes at the existence of God, at the basis of morals, at the hope of a future life, at the very idea of the supernatural. It cannot be an idle thing, in the presence of such an antagonist to Christian faith and hope, to look well to the foundations of our religious life, and learn how best to maintain the truth as it is in Jesus.

Isaac Errett.

WELCOME.

MOVED to joyousness by the glories of the earth around us and the heavens above us, by the blessings that are always coming from earth and air and sky, — lifted to thankfulness by the memory of a tender guidance along the better ways of life, by a glad appreciation of the present helpfulness of our Heavenly Father, — upheld by a hope that has for its foundation a knowledge of past and passing good, to us made grand by a faith that fails us not, we welcomed you to our city and our homes.

If we understand the object of this Lectureship, it is to discover and express what is true. No community, no church can be in more active sympathy with this endeavor. We are aware that every truth discovered in religion as in science, involves many failures, and, whether we believe more or less than others, we extend a hearty hand-shake and a greeting to every one that can say, "I also believe and therefore speak."

We welcome you because with you we have been led up a second Mount of Transfiguration, and have together heard from our divine leader, when breathing the spirit of his glorious life upon us. "You are the light of the world."

We welcome you the more gladly because of your religious profession considered from a scientific standpoint. Had you a creed to defend, human authorities to balance against each other, a confession of faith to champion, or a system of speculative philosophy with which to vex or mystify the world, we could have but small interest in your wranglings. But we greet you as Christians, endeavoring to discover naught else than Christian truth. Looking back you see no shrines built by human hands, at which you must kneel, no ruined temples which you must rebuild, no tombs at which you must bow down and weep, no oft besieged fortress of doubtful value, but which you must return to defend, but you see your banner always before you, and the voice of your Leader is always, "Forward."

Though claiming no more of wisdom, knowledge, honesty or zeal than is possessed by others, we may justly claim that we need to carry less of the dead weight of human opinions and human authority, and hence should be the better prepared for active, aggressive warfare in the field of conflict that lies before us.

Let us not delude ourselves with the idea that the battle for religious knowledge is half fought yet; only the skirmishers have commenced a desultory firing, and the boomings of cannon fired centuries apart tell where the strongholds of the enemy are. When man knew but little of the world's science, he thought but little; while his circle of light was small, his circumference of darkness was also small, and though his area of light has almost infinitely enlarged, beyond is an absolute infinitude of darkness, of which we can only say, "The spirit of God moves upon the face of its waters."

The movement of the human mind in the discovery of religious truth has been anything but constant or steady.

Every religious body on earth tells of a movement forward, a halt and a long discussion of things of doubtful value, or of a retrogression and a death; and to-day we have presented to us the sad and sickening spectacle of a waste of half the energies of the Christian world in a wrangling about things of no value to Christian life. Judaism, Mohammedanism, Catholicism, and every other ism on earth, is in a clear, and easily defined sense, the drift and debris that has been left by the flood of religious thought and feeling that has been bursting from the human heart and flowing onward toward God. Sometimes the flood sweeps one of the less of these away, but generally they grow larger and more formidable by the constant accumulation of human opinions, interests and authorities. One of the greatest mistakes made by the world's greatest religious thinkers, has been the appointment of unproved opinions as the ultimatum of truth. Shall we profit by the mistakes of these, or shall we repeat them? Shall we rush into and defend a fort cast up fifty years ago, and rally around a flag held by a dead hand, or shall we press forward to the mark of the prize of the high calling in Christ Jesus our Lord? Let us remember that Jesus Christ is not only yesterday and to-day, but also forever.

Again we welcome you.

A. E. HIGGASON.

THE RESPONSE was not furnished the publisher.

THE TWO REVELATIONS.

BY A. B. JONES.

"Having the eyes of your heart enlightened, that you may know what is the hope of your calling, what the riches of the glory of his inheritance in the saints." — Eph. 1:18, Revised Version.

THE heart has eyes and can see. The common version renders it, "the eyes of your understanding." In either case is involved the idea of man's intuitional nature in its relation to religion outwardly revealed.

Our safety lies in our fidelity to our spiritual intuitions. As the needle, when unobstructed, turns unerringly to the pole, so does the human soul, in its normal condition, turn to truth and to God. And as all truth is harmonious with itself, so is every moral being, when true to his own nature, in harmony with all truth. John Stewart Mill said: "There may be a world where two and two make five;" but to the man who believes in the God of the Bible the conception is impossible, as it not only puts rational natures in antagonism with truth, but antagonizes them with each other, and makes it impossible for them all to be in harmony with the Divine nature. There may be lower and higher, important and more important truths as there are lower and higher intelligencies; but unity of truth and unity of nature in all rational and moral life are essential ideas, at least in all religious thought.

Every moral being recognizing God as a creator and father, finds in the laws of his own nature a revelation of the Divine mind. Nor can the heavenly Father ever make to such a being an outward revelation that in any wise contradicts these laws, since there is no foundation on which the knowledge or faith of such revelation may stand. If, then, the Divine being has made to man an external revelation, it must be the correlative of man's moral and spiritual nature. That revelation must be to the " eyes of the heart," as the light of the sun is to the physical eye. We may here recall the teachings of Christ on this subject: " The light of the body is the eye; if, therefore, thine eye be single thy whole body shall be full of light; but if thine eye be evil, thy whole body shall be full of darkness. If, therefore, the light that is in thee be darkness, how great is that darkness!" " *The light that is in thee,*" refers to man's intuitional nature, which is to the soul as the eye is to the body, an original and essential part of the organism. The power of thought is not more certainly a part of human nature than is the power of moral distinctions; nor is either more distinct as an active force than the religious element. Man is a worshipper. Universal consciousness and universal history alike attest this. God having given to man this nature, it becomes his own witness. To this he appeals in making external revelations; and every such revelation must be subordinated to this *oracle within* in the sense that it must be addressed to man's spiritual understanding and be in accord with it.

But this spiritual nature is not infallible; like the powers of reason and moral distinctions it is liable to err, and needs to be guarded and assisted by outward revelation. But no external revelation can ever be infallible in its manward look. On its Godward side it may be so; but, being addressed to an imperfect nature through the medium of human speech, and having to be received and interpreted by a fallible being, practically it can never become to man an infallible revelation.

We speak of external revelation now as a whole, and in general terms. The great and fundamental matters of human duty and human conduct are so universally evolved in man's consciousness, in his normal condition; and so clearly revealed in the Scriptures, that we may suppose infallibility to be approximated, if not positively attained in this direction. "That those things which cannot be shaken may remain." Paul here intimates that there are some things common to all forms of religious thought and life, things essential in man's moral consciousness and in revelation; and which will survive the revolutions of theological dogmas and ecclesiasticisms, — things which "cannot be shaken." These are the "things" which the "eyes of the heart" see; these are the "things" which make "the light that is in you;" and these are the "things" in harmony with which every thought in the spheres of reason and revelation must be brought.

Men are beginning to understand that religion is no mystery, that it is no foreign element engrafted on the human soul, and that it is no mere impulse of the sympathetic nature. Religion is germinally involved in man's moral organization, is indigenous and spontaneous in the human heart; and to understand it we must first look within.

The Greeks consulted their oracles and waited for their revelations in the sighing of the winds, the noise of waterfalls, and other physical phenomena, to be interpreted by some expert specially called and qualified for the difficult and delicate task. The Romans had their Sibyline books which, at the instance of the great Senate, were consulted and expounded by professionals, while the gaping multitudes were taught to listen and receive these extraneous revelations with blind credulity. In striking contrast with these superstitious notions the great law-giver of Israel, Moses, said to that people, "this commandment which I command thee this day, it is not hidden from thee, neither is it far off. It is not in heaven that thou shouldst say, who shall go up for us to heaven and bring it unto us, that we may hear it and do it? Neither is it beyond the sea, that thou shouldst say, who shall go over the sea for us and bring it unto us that we may hear it and do it? But the word is very nigh unto thee, in thy mouth, and in thy heart, that thou mayest do it." And with these words before his mind the apostle, evidently, by indirect quotation, applies them substantially to the gospel of Jesus Christ. Hear him in his epistle to the Romans: "The righteousness which is of faith speaketh on this wise. Say not in thine heart who shall ascend into heaven that is to bring Christ down from above? or who shall descend into the deep that is to bring Christ up again from the dead? But what saith it? The word is nigh thee, even in thy mouth, and in thy heart, that is the word of faith which we preach."

The religions, then, of the Old Testament and of the New Testament, Judaism and Christianity, are declared by their chief expounders to be but *an outward and authoritative formulation of man's religious consciousness*. And, in view of this fact, it may be assumed that no man can ever understand the Scriptures except in the light of his own nature; nor can any man fully understand his own nature except in the light of the Scriptures. Both being revelations from God, and being correlated, they mutually interpret each other. They are to each other as the lecture-room and the dissecting-room of a medical university; as the psychology of the books and the psychology of the mind. It is our special object now to make this appear.

The religion of Moses is set forth elaborately in the Scriptures of the Old Testament. Large a book as it is, and profuse as are its teachings, and its ritualistic services, yet, by common consent, that whole system of religion is generically involved in the decalogue. Indeed, it may be claimed that our civilization is based upon the ten commandments; that its highest evolutions of moral and spiritual thought are originally and germinally in "the law written upon tables of stone." The line upon line, and the precept upon precept given by Moses and the prophets, as well as the detailed services of the priesthood, were only intended to unfold, illustrate and inculcate the great moral law. Analytically considered, then, the Jewish religion is resolved into the ten commandments. But these ten commandments may be further generalized. In reality they contain but *three great cardinal ideas*. The first regulates man's life in relation to God; the second regulates it in relation to the family; and the third in relation to society at large.

Four commandments of the decalogue are devoted to the elaboration of the first thought: —

1. " Thou shalt have no other gods before me."
2. " Thou shalt not make unto thee any graven image."
3. " Thou shalt not take the name of the Lord thy God in vain."
4. " Remember the Sabbath day to keep it holy."

It is evident that these commandments all point to the one great idea of the soul's allegiance and supreme homage to the one true and living God. No other God, nor any graven image, is allowed to come between man and his heavenly Father. His holy name is to be held in profound reverence; and to promote these ends, one day of the week is set apart wherein the mind and body are to be given rest from worldly occupations, and the soul to have opportunity to renew itself by meditation and worship before the Lord. The simple thought, then, that man should render to the Supreme Being the highest suffrages of the soul, is the one vital conception of these four commandments.

But this disposition is inherent in man's nature. The universal prevalence among the nations and tribes of the earth of religious ideas, and the universal tendency of men to worship the Deity, in some form or other, indicate that this principle is constitutional with man; and that this external law is but the counterpart of that which God hath previously inscribed upon the tablets of the heart. "When the Gentiles, which have not the law, do by nature the things contained in the law, these, having not the law, are a law unto themselves; which show the work of the law *written in their hearts.*"

In a similar manner we observe the second fundamental idea of the decalogue, that of the family eliminated in the following commandments: —

1. "Thou shalt not commit adultery."
2. "Honor thy father and thy mother."

But may it not be said in regard to these two laws that " nature itself teaches that it is a shame " to live otherwise? They are but the formal declarations of man's instincts. The very loves and jealousies of the human heart in its filial and sexual relations clearly indicate that this part of the great moral law is likewise a part of human nature. And the fact that men have sometimes taught and practiced differently does not set aside the fact that the family idea, as here set forth, is both the human and the divine conception — both the law of nature and the law of God. There is, perhaps, no principle, human or divine, that has not been abused, perverted and ignored by men. But it is a fact verified by history that as men return from their moral wanderings, and as they recover themselves from their lapsed conditions of ignorance and depravity, and are evolved into higher civilizations, they come to the conscious recognition of this Divine idea of the family, where one man and one woman live in perpetual fidelity to each other; and where children honor their parents, as nature's law, and the heart's own proclamation.

But provision is made in the law given from Sinai for the regulation of man's life as a citizen, as a member of society. This third and last fundamental idea, underlying the religion of Moses, involves these four subordinate principles: (*a*) Veracity; (*b*) the right of property; (*c*) the right of life, and (*d*) that character is not determined simply by overt acts, but by the condition of the heart as well, which principles are formally announced in the remaining four commandments of the decalogue: —

1. "Thou shalt not steal."
2. "Thou shalt not kill."
3. "Thou shalt not bear false witness."
4. "Thou shalt not covet."

Here again we observe that the requirements of the revealed law are echoed by the conscience or moral sense of man. That they are essentially right, in the nature of things, is the universal verdict of mankind; and the human mind is so organized that it can never, in its normal condition, conceive of these principles otherwise than as they are, — just and right. Did any human being ever violate these laws in their true spirit and meaning, without a consequent sense of wrong and guilt and unworthiness? Is it possible for us to conceive of a society of men so organized that a disregard of these fundamental ideas of the moral law would be a virtue, would result in moral excellence, or contribute to their welfare? Is not a violation of the law written upon the tables of stone, a violation of the law of man's moral constitution? "This commandment which I command thee this day, it is not hidden from thee, neither is it far off. It is not in heaven, that thou shouldst say, who shall go up for us to heaven, and bring it unto us, that we may have it, do it? Neither is it beyond the sea, that thou shouldst say, who shall go over the sea for us and bring it unto us, that we may hear it and do it? But the word is *very nigh unto thee in thy mouth and in thy heart*, that thou mayst do it."

Turning now to the New Testament scriptures and adopting somewhat the same method of investigation, we shall reach a similar conclusion in reference to Christianity as a system of revealed truth. The gospel, or as Paul styles it, the "Word of Faith," or the "Righteousness of Faith," is the *supplement* of the law. Not that the law was in itself defective, or in any wise a failure on its own account, but it needed to be supplemented in consequence of the weakness of men. "The law was weak through the flesh," and hence God supplemented it by "sending his own Son in the likeness of sinful flesh." As a rule of life for man in his threefold relation to God, the family, and society, it was ample and adequate in its provisions had men been faithful to it. The apostle Paul says, "The law is holy, and the commandment holy, and just and good." Again he says: "I delight in the law of God after the inward man," showing not only that the law is good in itself, but that the harmony observed between it and the mind is so complete as to create "delight" in the soul. This supplemental religion of the New Testament may be generalized according to its fundamental thoughts very much as the Old Testament scriptures have been. Christianity comes to the world with three postulates. It assumes in the first place that men are *sinners:* secondly, that there is a consequent necessity of Divine *toleration*, and, thirdly, a necessity of Divine *aid*. These things are assumed for the reason that their formal proof is unnecessary. In the presence of that law which is " holy, just, and good," every man pleads guilty of sin. While the " inward man" "delights in the law" theoretically, yet he "sees another law warring against the law of the mind," and bringing the man into "captivity;" who from the depths of his spiritual humiliation, cries out, " O, wretched man that I am!" In addition to this, the man sees with the " eyes of the heart" his own helplessness in the presence of that violated law, and exclaims again, "Who shall deliver me?" SIN, TOLERATION, ASSISTANCE, — these words are indicative of the condition of man's moral consciousness universally. But these words also indicate the spirit and meaning of the gospel of Jesus Christ. It is a message of "peace and good will." "Thou shalt call his name Jesus; for he shall save his people from their sins." The doctrine of the forgiveness of sins through the forbearance of God is fundamental to the gospel.

But this is not sufficient to meet the wants of the impaired soul. The failure of the past, the consequent weakness and infirmity of the present, forewarn it of its inability to keep that law in the future. Hence the promise of assistance in this spiritual struggle. This aid is guaranteed to us, firstly, *in a fuller revelation of truth;* secondly, *in the gift of the Holy Spirit;* thirdly, *in the fellowships of an associated church life.*

The fundamental principles of the "law which came by Moses" underlie the whole system of "grace and truth which came by Jesus Christ." Man properly adjusted in his relations to God, to the family, and to society — these principles are identical in the Old Testament and in the New; but these germinal thoughts have been recast and expanded; fuller measures of light have fallen upon them, and new angles of vision from which to view them have been discovered. As great seed truths they have, under these more favorable conditions of after ages, grown up, "first the blade, then the ear, after that the full corn in the ear." This additional light falling upon the mind has gratefully aided the soul in its battle with sin. But this is not all. The Holy Spirit is given to the child of God to carry on this work of confirmation. The Savior said: "If I go away, I will send the Comforter unto you." And again, it is said: "He shall be in you," "He shall abide with you forever," "He shall guide" and "seal" you, be an "earnest of your inheritance," make "intercession" for you, and "strengthen you with might in the inner man," — all of which are "exceeding great and precious promises," and are to the weak and weary soul, hungering and thirsting after righteousness, as the water brooks are to the panting hart. And to further meet our conscious needs and promote our spiritual growth and well being, the people of God have been "called out" from the world and organically disengaged from their alliance with the state, as under the reign of Judaism. They are "called unto the fellowship of the saints," and organically associated as the "church of the living God," as a "kingdom not of this world," as members of the "one body" and "members one of another." In this purely spiritual relation there are special advantages and opportunities for mutual sympathy and aid in the divine life. Here, unaffected by the accidental distinctions of this earthly life, they are "all of one spirit;" "the strong carry the infirmities of the weak," "weeping with those that weep, and rejoicing with those that rejoice," "bearing one another's burdens, and so fulfilling the law."

In Christianity, then, as in Judaism, there is a perfect adjustment of the outer revelations to the inner life of man. The proclamations of the law and of the gospel are heard alike by every man as the "voice of one crying in the wilderness" of his heart. And, hence, the apostle catches the refrain from the prophet "the righteousness which of faith" (that is the gospel) "speaketh on this wise, say not in thine heart who shall ascend into heaven that is to bring Christ down" (that is the Christ idea), "or who shall descend into the deep to bring up Christ again from the dead? But what saith it? The word is nigh thee, even in thy mouth, and in thy heart; that is the word of faith which we preach." No wonder, then, that the shepherds gave such ready response to the heavenly message, " Behold, I bring you good tidings of great joy, which shall be to all people. For unto you is born this day, in the city of David, a Savior, which is Christ the Lord." Is it any matter of surprise that " it came to pass, as the angels were gone away from them into heaven, the shepherds said, one to another, let us now go even unto Bethlehem, and see this thing which is come to pass, which the Lord hath made known unto us?" May we not rather be amazed that all men do not yield the same prompt answer to this message of love and peace?

Christ is the embodiment of this law, and of this gospel. In his life and death he arrays before the world, in glowing colors, the fundamental conceptions of both, and presses them home to the conscience as is possible in no other way. By faithfully observing the requirements of the law, he illustrates and vindicates its claims before the world; and by the painful contrast in his own faultless life and ours he quickens the moral sense of man with the consciousness of his own sinfulness in not keeping that law which is potentially " in his heart," and theoretically approved " in his mouth." Why the universal admiration of the character of Jesus Christ? The most distinguished opposer of Christianity of the present age has eloquently said: " I give to the man Christ Jesus the homage of my admiration and my tears." Why so? Because " this commandment " embodied in Jesus is not "hidden" from men, but is the true exposition, and the righteous interpretation of what is within them.

In the life of Christ we also have a revelation of sin. Without that life men could never have fully understood the desperate nature and the real sinfulness of sin. While the lights about them were sufficient to awaken a sense of guilt, yet the vast possibility of the "law of the members, warring against the law of the mind," and completely overriding the "inward man," extinguishing "the light that is in him," and leaving the soul morally eclipsed, and in total darkness, — all this was not understood. Were a people to propose now to obliterate the whole moral law, which, as already observed, constitutes not only the foundation of the religions of both Old and New Testaments, but of our very civilization as well, they would be looked upon as the pronounced enemies of both God and men. But this is substantially what was proposed in the crucifixion of Jesus Christ, who was the personification of that law. And when the multitude cry out, "Away with him! Crucify him! crucify him!" the awful nature and boundless possibilities of sin are discovered to us. Furthermore, Christ is the embodiment and revelation of sin in that he "made his soul an offering for sin." He died on account of sin and in behalf of sinners. This tragic event has turned the course of the world's thought on the subject of sin. The public conscience has become enlightened and quickened both with a sense of guilt and with an inspiration for deliverance from its thralldom. That

Christ was the embodiment of the ideas of Divine toleration and assistance needs not to be argued. The whole current of his teachings and his life flow uninterruptedly in that direction. His words were the words of comfort and mercy; his acts were acts of deliverance and salvation. Sins were forgiven; the sick were relieved; the dead were raised up, and the tear of sorrow was staid. Thus we perceive in Jesus of Nazareth the symbol not only of the Divine love, but the symbol of Divine thought.

The moral conceptions of God heretofore revealed through oral instruction and legislative enactments are transferred to a life. God says: "Behold him! This is what I mean; this is what I have been trying to teach you for centuries." Hence, he is the "Word" of God, the sign and expression of·the Divine idea. He is also the sign and expression of the human idea. He is both Divine and human; and the mediator between God and man; the one in whom meet and blend both the external and the internal revelations of the Father; in whom all the fundamental thoughts of the law and·of the gospel find their most eloquent utterance, and the whole spiritual consciousness of man finds its most perfect expression.

If, now, it be true that this external revelation of God in the Old and New Testament scriptures be identical with His internal revelations in human consciousness, *where the necessity of the external revelation?* In the fearful contest between the flesh and the spirit man needs to have his spiritual nature reinforced. The "carnal mind" is so closely allied with the objects of physical sense immediately around it, the rewards of its efforts come so directly and accumulate so rapidly that the authority of the higher spiritual nature is constantly in danger of being disregarded in the heat of the passions, and its voice suppressed amid the clamor of the appetites. The "natural man" needs no assistance in the prosecution of his work; the counterpart of his life is all around him; while the "spiritual man" "looking not at the things which are seen, but at the things which are unseen," needs to have his counterpart in the form of an authoritative, external revelation of truth, that in the mouth of two witnesses his faith may be confirmed, and his life established. This outward revelation is to the "hidden man of the heart" as the staff that supports the unsteady steps of the feeble man; or, better still, it is to the "eyes of the heart" as glasses are to our physical eyes, it serves to magnify and make more distinct the objects of our view, and to focalize our vision. It is a thought like this in the mind of the apostle when he said to his Ephesian brethren, "I cease not to give thanks for you, making mention of you in my prayers, that the God of our Lord Jesus Christ, the Father of glory, may give unto you the spirit of wisdom and revelation in the knowledge of him; having the eyes of your heart enlightened, that you may know what is the hope of his calling, what the riches of the glory of his inheritance in the saints, and what the exceeding greatness of his power to us-ward who believe."

It need scarcely be said that without this outward and authoritative revelation from God to support and reinforce the "spiritual man" in his unequal contest with the "natural man," that the battle is a hopeless one and defeat is inevitable. "The whole creation" would indeed be left to "groan and travail in pain together," unable to give birth and life to its brightest and best thoughts. The "struggle" of Jacob and Esau is perpetual in the womb of humanity, and whenever deliverance comes, Esau is always the first born and the elder brother. And as Jacob eventually obtained the blessing through the favor of his mother, so must the spiritual man conquer by the grace of God.

Finally, let it be observed that this happy correspondence between the inner and the outer revelations of truth is the very *ground of our faith*. It is the only foundation on which we can build. Exclude that and the establishment of religion becomes an impossibility. No rational man can believe in God and yet believe that he is arbitrary in his nature, that he approaches men through forms of thought or legislative enactments contradictory of what is essentially a part of man's nature. There is evidently a vast space that separates the finite from the infinite; but, whenever the Infinite One enters the sphere of the finite there must be unity of thought, or man can never be God's child. On this basis is founded the internal evidences of religion, which in reality constitute the everlasting temple of our faith, while the external evidences stand as the scaffolding of the inner structure. And this power of the soul to see and to know the truth in the present conditions of its alliance with the flesh, and its consequent unfavorable environment, is a sublime prophecy of its future glorification when it shall no longer " know in part," " when that which is in part shall be done away," when the days and years of its childhood have been past, and the royal dignities of manhood have been attained, when it shall no longer " see through a glass darkly, but face to face," and " know even as it is known."

Of all the grand possibilities open to the human soul, that of its own complete enfranchisement in the realm of truth is the grandest. "You shall know the truth," says Jesus, " and the truth shall make you free." The possibility of establishing the " kingdom of God within you," of transferring the external law to the sphere of the inner life so far as to lose all consciousness of outward authority, and yet, to move forever onward and upward amid the harmonies of a divine and endless life — this possibility is before every man.

DISCUSSION ON A. B. JONES' PAPER.

J. H. Hughes asked how the essayist would reconcile what he said with Paul's statement: " I had not known lust, except the law had said ' Thou shalt not covet.' " (Rom. vii: 7.) It seems to me, said he, that this is opposed to the idea of such knowledge being in the soul.

J. H. Foy spoke of Seneca, Confucius, Socrates and Pythagoras teaching many of the same truths Jesus enforced, and thought, therefore, that there might be some truth in what the essayist said. However, said he, on the other side, there is Paul's declaration that "the natural man receiveth not the things of the spirit of God." (1 Cor. ii: 14).

M. M. Goode said if he understood the address he indorsed it. It was true the world by wisdom knew not God, yet it had the conditions of knowing him when he was presented.

T. P. Haley commended the essay. The thoughts were clear and distinct. The essayist, however, was unfortunate in wording his theme. It should not be said that there are two revelations from God. What is a revelation? If all that was presented in the essay as belonging to the "internal" revelation were in the soul of a man there would be little need of an external revelation. It is a singular revelation that God has revealed himself in the intuitions of the men of this world. I have been reading Freeman Clarke's "Ten Great Religions" lately, and I do not think anything mentioned therein as belonging to these religions is from God except in a very corrupted condition, as having been received by tradition. It is not fair to take what we find in the consciousness of men trained in Christian truth and which *responds* to this, and declare it to be a primary oracle. God has made the soul for truth as the eye for light, and he sends man his revelation to fulfil the soul's demands. Because I recognize duties citizen-ward or family-ward does it follow that God first revealed these to me, as a primary oracle, through my soul? I had rather believe that God made man with a capacity to receive his message, and then communicated it to him through the organs ordained to this end.

G. R. Hand said: Light was let into a house to reveal what was within. I thought I went along with the essayist when he spoke of God's word shining upon his works; but when he specified the soul, stating that all its knowledge was primary — the result of its own effort — I didn't so well know whether I could indorse it. You may go to nature to find corroborations, but not to find revelations. Those Athenians to whom Paul preached certainly failed to find these revelations in the soul the essayist speaks of, because he states that "the times of this *ignorance* God winked at," not these *revelations*.

A. Proctor said: It is a debate of definitions. One says "intuitions," the other "revelations." God constituted the human soul so that it wants truth. While the world was wrestling with its thought of the Deity, exerting its imagination to the utmost stretch, until it had created a thousand gods, Moses came along declaring "There is one God." But he couldn't get them to see that, neither could the prophets and judges. After a while Socrates came along, and he confirmed Moses' view. Now where did Socrates get his thought? And why should his thought be like Moses' thought, which came from God? God and man are one in nature. They have the same natures. Both think, love, understand alike. So we think along similar lines.

E. B. Cake asked: Is there anything in the essay for him? Intuition, what is it? Tuition in. It is teaching in. It is a reality. There is a hunger and thirst which the soul possesses for truth, and God supplies it. The soul is the greatest thing in the universe. God talks to himself when he talks to man.

J. A. Brooks did not believe that Confucius gave the world the Golden Rule, or that Socrates spoke those wondrous things mentioned this morning, because they were revelations of the soul. Had there not come whisperings from the hoary past? Was not tradition able to bring men the thoughts of God spoken ages ago? It may be God inspired these men as he did others, but certainly they did not produce these glorious truths unaided by the Divine mind. I do not believe that our highest civilization sprang from Judaism. This is to go back to the twilight. Take away the revelation of Jesus Christ, and what does man amount to?

J. H. Foy said, in response to the previous speaker, that, although it was the Jews who had the revelation of God, it was the Greeks who responded most heartily to the gospel call, showing thereby that there must have been some value attaching to these truths they had wrought out.

J. W. Monser said he was very much pleased with the essay. Its careful qualifications rendered it almost faultless. His only criticism would be this: He thought the essayist wrong in asserting that the highest civilization springs from Judaism. Lecky, and other rationalistic writers, even, do not so view the matter. They consider that the spontaneity and sacrifice inculcated by Christianity to be the prime causes of our best culture. He thought that more credit ought to be given to the cross.

O. C. Hill wholly agreed with the essayist. He thought he understood him. When a man realizes the grand possibilities within him that is a revelation to him. Man, in the unfolding of his spirit, has found out what God has revealed. The essayist taught the threefold relationship to family, citizen, and God, and that the gospel is but the flowering out of these.

R. L. Lotz said: If there is to be a revelation, there must be some being to whom it is to be made. The Spirit is that entity. How, then, can it be a revelation itself? He does not think that because man is imperfect that the revelation was imperfect. The Savior was perfect, but still suited to imperfect man. If I have an eye I must have something to see. God must give me something to see. Power to see and a revelation in the soul are two different things.

J. A. Lord said: If the essayist is right about correlations, what will he do with the gospel while it was a mystery, or even now, when it is a mystery to any one? There is nothing in such case to correlate with this "inner revelation" of the essayist. Further, it seems to me the essayist misapplies Paul's statement as found in Rom. x: 8–10. The word there, in the heart, is the gospel which was preached, and one of the truths in the heart was "that God hath raised him from the dead." How could such a truth as this be a primary oracle of the soul? It is not a truth that can be wrought out in the soul so as to be made conscious to us.

A. B. JONES' REJOINDER.

He said that so many points had been raised it was not easy to remember them all, nor could he well reply to so much in the short time allowed for closing the discussion. Much said by the speakers was quite foreign to the matter of the essay, while there were some points made by some of the speakers that were pertinent, and deserving of notice. The chief matter of difference between him and those dissenting from his views, as expressed in the essay, is in the *nature and possibilities of the human mind*. His critics seem to think the mind incapable of thinking at all, or at least of thinking correctly, on moral and religious questions until it is moved upon by some higher intelligence. That had Adam treated Eve with the utmost consideration and kindness she would never have thought of his conduct as having the moral quality of goodness unless God had first told her that she had a very kind and good husband; nor had he practised toward his wife the greatest cruelty, even pulling out her eyes, would she, of herself, have ever complained that his behavior was morally wrong. That the original man and woman in Eden would never have lifted a thought in reverence toward the Supreme Being, unless the Supreme Being had first came to them in the form of an outward, verbal revelation. Upon the other hand, the essayist holds that the soul of a man, by virtue of its own organization, when placed in its normal, earthly relations, is capable of moral and spiritual thought. That there is lodged in the mind a force that works from within outward; that its nature is such as not only enables it to receive impressions from oral revelations, but that it has the capacity, when touched by the influences of its ordinary earthly environment, of evolving thought, true and noble thought, from within itself.

While his dissenting critics looked upon the spiritual nature of man as a piece of marble, which may be wrought into form and beauty by the hand and chisel of the artist, he preferred to liken it to a seed that has involved in it a measure of life and force which, in its ordinary relations to the earth, the atmosphere and the sunbeams, will grow and develop of itself, without the aid of cultivation. It is not denied that this assistance from the hand of industry without will promote the better growth and maturity of the seed; nor is it denied that the inspired verbal revelation greatly assists the human mind in reaching just conclusions on all moral and religious questions.

The objection urged by Brother Hughes to the doctrine of the essay founded on Paul's statement that he "would not have known lust except the law had said, thou shalt not covet," resolves itself simply into this: That without this outward revelation he would not have known the sin of lust as he *now* knows it; his ideas on this moral subject would not have reached such maturity, or been rounded out in such perfection.

Brother Lord objects to the interpretation of Paul's teaching in the tenth chapter of Romans, on the ground that he names the resurrection of Christ as one of the items of the gospel which is to be believed, and the doctrine of the resurrection is not intuitive. Of course it is not. What the essayist maintains is that the fundamental ideas underneath the resurrection, and other incidental facts of the gospel — the ideas of sin on the part of man, of toleration and assistance on the part of God, are original moral conceptions of the human mind. The life, death, and resurrection of Jesus Christ are means employed on the part of the heavenly Father to meet and satisfy the demands of of these deep, spiritual intuitions. Hence Paul says, "the word is nigh thee;" the fundamental ideas of the gospel are intuitive, "the word of faith which we preach," so that if you will "confess with your mouth the Lord Jesus and believe in your heart that God raised him from the dead," that is, if you will accept of the outward facts through which this divine toleration and aid is revealed, "you shall be saved."

Brother Haley thinks the title of the essay not a happy one. In this he may be correct. The essayist is not so much concerned about the title as he is about the subject matter: and yet he thinks the title "THE TWO REVELATIONS," serves him a good purpose. It serves to arrest attention and awaken interest in the discussion of a most important scriptural theme. The essayist does not hold that there are two revelation bringing to us two different systems of truth, or two moral theories on any subject. "THE TWO REVELATIONS" simply means that there are two methods by which God makes known to man essential fundamental truth. The laws of man's rational and moral nature, whereby he perceives truth, is one method; the Bible, in which the Spirit of God formulates thought, and appeals to the human understanding through words as the signs of ideas, is another method. While the methods are two, the truth is ever one and the same. We have "THE TWO REVELATIONS" of the one glorious system of divine truth.

THE ORIGIN AND PROGRESS OF FREE THOUGHT.

This address, given first orally, has since been revised, and new matter added.

BY J. W. MONSER.

OUR first concern is to settle what we mean when we use the term "free thought." Words, by usage, become historical, and therefore to take them after they have acquired a technical sense, applying such primitive meanings as belong to them before their appropriation to special ends, is to introduce debate where we desire unity of thought. The words, *free thought*, in their simplest sense are applicable alike to every system and school, being merely indicative of that liberty which belongs as an inalienable right to the mind. Christians and infidels are alike and equally free to think, and the fact that one is readier to assert that right than the other, or more frequent in his defence of it, is no proof that it is in his exclusive possession. It is in the technical sense, then, that we have to do with these words — the sense in which those who claim them are specifically denominated thereby — that sense in which the world recognizes these words as having peculiar point and reference.

Special significance began to attach to the word, *freethinker*, about the end of the seventeenth century.

Molyneux in a letter to Locke characterizes Toland as "a candid free thinker." Shaftesbury, in 1709, speaks of "our modern free writers," referring to certain latitudinarian minds (see Works, vol. I., p. 65). And Collins, in 1713, in his *Discourse of Free Thinking*, first appropriated the name to express the independence of inquiry which was claimed by deists. It will not be questioned, I think, that since then these words have possessed a specific meaning. Certainly one never expects to hear them applied to any but those who are supposed to question the Bible's absolute authority. How it comes about that such schools of thought exist will now employ our attention.

In the treatment of this theme we can choose either the historical method, presenting ideas and facts in something like a chronological order; or we can enter examination of the causes that have led to the present proportions of freethinking. We prefer the latter. These causes, as we observe them, are to be divided into three classes: Intellectual, Political, and Religious. Under the head of Intellectual we note these sub-classes: Modes of mental action and phases of thought. This leads us to consider, first of all, modes of mental action, the characteristic most observable, being collision. In our pursuit after knowledge there are two methods of research, the experimental and the historic. The experimental, is by necessity, a process pursued originally, and hence, independently, the individual in quest of information, availing himself of inductions, as he acquires and classifies his facts. This is looked upon as an experimental method because the pursuer rests on no previous acquisitions. The historic method is more conservative in its course. It may, indeed, be critical, but its dealing is with that already obtained. It rests on testimony, forming conclusion from the weight of evidence. Practically, each of these complements the other. The experimental is forlorn, indeed, if it declines all aid from that, which once *truly* experimental, became, as a consequence, historic. So, the historic, becomes suicidal in its action, if it cuts off its sources in the experimental. As it is, out of these spring two authorities; the authority of current thought and the authority of dogma. The abuse of these authorities is productive of mischief. While the one speculates and opinionates, is restless and eager to push on: the other, receives and pronounces, is stationary and roots itself down.

The progress of mankind is itself an incidental cause of free thought. The introduction of anything new in the realm of thought, whether secular, social, or religious, tends to the production of consternation on the part of many. Each age has its accepted and approved system, and if this system had its weaknesses, the masses, feel with Hamlet, it is better to cling to those we have, than fly to others that we know not of. The very attempt to question it is suggestive of "dangerous doubt." The present strengthened with all the resources of the past, is wholly sufficient for many. They live for no future. Their eyes are always turned back on the clock of history. Prophecy — a reaching forth into the rich and unexplored future — has no inspiration for them. Now, it is evident that

THE ORIGIN AND PROGRESS OF FREE THOUGHT. 37

dealing with such a quick and stirring world as ours, this sort of conservatism must be a constant generator of its opposite progression. Not to take into account, as an important factor, the inevitable tendency of the mind to fly from one extreme to the other, an act that seems purely involuntary, and belonging to the necessity of things — such conduct, as we note above sets up processes of investigations, if not inspired by a spirit of retaliation, at least occasioned by a fear lest too stringent restrictions shall be placed on human thought. Historically considered, we are bound to date almost every important outbreak of infidelity back to such epochs as are marked for disinclination to admit current but well-attested facts. Collisions like these produce jealousies and induce the entrance of vicious elements. Scholarly pride chafes at the bit, bursts its harness, and dashes away wildly, having no regard to what lies in its course.

There are ages and seasons when the human mind busies itself in exploring the origin of things. Mystery upon mystery, heaps upon heaps, present themselves. The legion of relationship, sustained by the inhabitants and substances of this universe to each other, provoke question and call for answer. This may not be true with respect to the dormant and easily satisfied mass of men. But it is with respect to the inquisitive. Such minds are pioneers to national culture. Out and away from barbarism we are brought by contemplating the origin and destiny of things. There is no harm in such a use of the mind. As long as honest methods of induction are pursued and the bounds of legitimate inquiry are observed good profits are realized. But if palpable facts are spurned, and the investigator becomes intolerant of the world of realities — if he becomes vainly puffed up and intrudes into the realm of the unseen — instead of a helper of men, he may become a most unmitigated hindrance.

Two evils we mark in thinkers worthy of your attention. One, to give oneself over to thinking in a mere professional way, having no well-defined object before one, thinking because of the joy that comes with discovery. Coleridge and DeQuincey were types of this class, in England; and one can hardly pick amiss if he blindfolds himself, selecting Germany as a field. The other evil, is that of taking a fundamental proposition out of its connection and category, and twisting it in to serve other and hostile interests. Such an instance is that of using Mansel's statement concerning the absolute and relative, with respect to God, in the service of evolution, as is done by Herbert Spencer. Either of these methods ("if that can be called shape which shape has none") is essentially destructive of mental integrity. The mind is not a plaything to toss to and fro, or to whirl into the air like a ball. It must have an object before it. It should have aim, and think toward a goal. Thought, to have force, must be definite. Fond of liberty as it may be, it must not ignore standards of measurement if it would attain to true climaxes. And above all else it must be honest in its dealings. Mental juggleries are abominated in the eyes of all good men.

Vast contradictions have occurred by an unfortunate

mixture of mental philosophies. Men whose humor it was to give precedence to the doctrine of intuitions, feeling rightly, that one's innate ideas were bound to obtain respect, felt embarrassed by their inability to harmonize these views with much that appertained to justly recognized, external teachings. Trained to regard these latter with reverence, and disinclined to relinquish what to them had become the same as moral axioms, their effort has been to compromise, by sandwiching the one with the other. It has been supposed by them that the exigency of the case demanded some such treatment. The great anxiety being to save what is valuable, it is thought wiser to take this course than to surrender all. The spirit of such thinkers is conservative of the old truths whilst it sympathizes with the new. A. S. Farrar, in his review of Coleridge's philosophy, says: " In looking backwards he seeks to discover what mankind has meant by their beliefs; in looking round he asks what are the elements which the present generation disapproves, and wishing to eliminate the error of the past, and appropriate the truth of the present, he looks inward into the human heart, and thinks he perceives a faculty there which unveils to man the eternal, absolute truth." This faculty, known as " the intuitional," becomes the guide of the light of which one is supposed to be able to thread his way through every system of thought, ancient, mediæval and modern; social, philosophical and religious. Some, seeing clearly whither the road leads, have shot along it at all hazards, while others halt dubiously at intermediate posts, fearful to move on to the advanced stations. Some of those who felt strong upon their first embracing of this philosophy, accepting their intuitions as absolute, and conceiving the conclusions drawn therefrom infallible, now seem inclined to modify their views, declaring these inner pronunciations to be capable of error. During this period of hesitancy it may be well to investigate a thing or two respecting intuitions. First, then, while we would delight in limiting our inquiry to the purely philosophical field, feeling assured that even here we should find food enough for thought, our space compels us at once to proceed with such examination as shall discover the relation of intuitions to revealed religion. In doing so, we shall allow Theodore Parker place, as a leading American exponent of this doctrine. He says, "This theory teaches that there is a natural supply for spiritual as well as corporal wants; that there is a connection between God and the soul, as between light and the eye, sound and the ear, food and the palate, truth and the intellect, beauty and the imagination."[1] The fallacy in all this consists in making the religious principle in man find its proper object in the same way that the senses find theirs. Two things are here confounded: the capacity for *receiving* religious truth, and the capacity of unaided reason to *discover* it. When Mr. Parker says: "We have spiritual faculties to lay hold on God and supply spiritual wants and through them we obtain all needed spiritual things," as he does in this same discourse, he practically cuts off all need

---

[1] Discourse on Religion, p. 160.

of supernatural provision. Do men obtain peace of conscience as easily and as naturally as their eyes obtain light? Do spiritual faculties and spiritual objects come together in this natural way? Each animal, in its natural state and pursuit attains its legitimate end, but does man? Here his analogy fails. Mr. Parker tells us further on that "for the religious consciousness of man, a knowledge of two great truths is indispensable: namely, a knowledge of the existence of an infinite God, and of the duty we owe Him." These, he holds, may be known independently of all revelation and supernatural aid by intuition and reflection. Still further on, he permits his system to take its attitude towards Christianity thus: "It bows to no idols, neither the church, nor the Bible, nor yet Jesus, but God only. * * * Its redeemer is within — its salvation within; its heaven and its oracle of God."[1]

Here then, we are placed face to face with this "inner light" and are enabled to estimate it at its actual value. One can readily see the comfort it affords infidelity. Declaring that "Christianity is dependent on no outside authority,"[2] it denies the historical truth of the Scriptures; and averring that "we verify its eternal truth in our soul," it relieves the miraculous of all necessary service. The firmer men have held to the intuitional philosophy the laxer have they been in their grasp of Biblical truths. More fascinating as a system than its opposite, the school of materialism, its influence has been subtler if not as

---

[1] Discourse on Religion, p. 361.
[2] Same, p. 209.

widely spread. Its substitution of a poetic philosophy for the system of redemption has blinded men from the discovery of their enormous loss; whereas, in the reception of bald, atheistic negations, the barrenness and void of the heart is so palpable, men quickly awake to a consciousness of their folly. That the intuitional philosophy does not take with the masses like some other more meager systems is because of its intricacy of idea; and yet this very intricacy may and does become the prolific cause of mental confusion, especially when it is espoused and propagated by those whose hearts are still too loyal towards God's revealed truth, to do more than entangle themselves occasionally, in their effort to do justice to whichever system they may, at the time, conceive to shed forth the truest light.

After a careful perusal of what men have said on this and kindred subjects, and a somewhat careful examination of their attempts to construct a true basis for humanity, we are constrained to believe that only those can hope to succeed who select a standard of thought and keep to it. Mental inconsistencies can result but in philosophical failures. No man but a clown can well straddle two horses at the same time, and an ox and mule do not yoke well together. If a man believes that the intentional, or any other philosophy, meets man's religious wants, by giving freedom and play to such eternal truths as his soul may seek to utter, let him adhere to this, alone, not jumbling it with something whose nature it is to vex, and give dismay to his philosophy. Time and trial will tell the story. If, on the contrary, he adheres to the belief that he knows nothing as he ought, and that it is from God's revealed message to man that his wisdom is to be drawn, let him be consistent, and give *this* his exclusive attention. He will find himself able to spare more philosophy than he had dreamed of, nor will he be seriously embarrassed in endeavoring to comprehend God's meaning. The time has come for the recognition of a visible standard. Men, as respects the Bible, are either for or against God. Differ as they may concerning interpretations, if they be Christians, they should at least keep their thoughts within the limits of Holy Writ, casting all their influence upon the side of the prophets and apostles. And who will dare say that even their very grossest conceptions are are not infinitely better than those of the men who despise the Bible and regard not God.

Having taken this brief survey of the intellectual field, we turn now to the political. Here we are to note such causes as spring from misalliances between church and state: revolutions of thought brought about by the dethronement of constituted authorities; together with such disaffections as result from the inequalities of society. The examination of this field transfers us to European territory. It is thence that much of the free thought we are dealing with has sprung. The domination of state churches has wrought ruin to the Christian religion, not only by the earthly caricatures they have made of the heavenly original, but also by the ecclesiastic tyrannies that have been issued and sustained by their hierarchies. A national intolerance, protected by the sanctities and authority of an espoused religion, is the most odious and insufferable of all intolerances. People can in some sort escape the oppressions of independent churches. They may refuse all affiliation or countenance. But there is no riddance but expatriation for the citizen whose very laws are originated by the cardinals or bishops, and enforced by the crown. The spirit of humanity, if it be not wholly enslaved, rises up against this. Such is the influence of it upon many as to involve in one unbroken flood of disgust everything assuming the shape or wearing the name of Christianity. The system of Christ is too paltry for consideration, in the estimation of a reflective mind, if it needs any such support. Men who seem ignorant of the Word of God have an inkling that on no such basis as this did Christianity arise. The preferment of bishoprics, and the division of the lands into dioceses and parishes, the impartial taxation of the inhabitants, irrespective of faith or non-faith, and the stringent enforcement of all national measures in the interests of the state church have been industrious propagators of free thought. While Italy and other Catholic countries have panted to shake off Popery, England and Ireland have panted to dislodge the Episcopacy. Even their most pretentious adherents are frequently honeycombed with doubts; their secret but crafty satires being a criterion of the heart's condition. Nothing can be worse than a bastard Christianity. It hoodwinks, robs and despoils the nation it feeds on. Its influence festers as it flies, and poisons that on which it reposes. It may be cheerfully said, to the credit of these churches, that within their own ranks are found hosts of valiant, true men, as eagerly bent on the destruction of these great evils as those outside.

The fortunes and misfortunes of nations, as developed by war, the change of dynasties, and such revolutions as are incidental to an excited and feverish people, go far towards the introduction of doubt. Perhaps in no important political revolution, — such, for example, as those under Cromwell, Napoleon and Washington, — has there been perfect immunity from skepticism. The minds of the masses are so constructed by the tutorage they have undergone, that the dethronement of constituted authority is generally attended with moral evil. When humanity is broken loose from its moorings danger is imminent. The greater the burden and tyranny heretofore, the larger the license taken afterwards. Nor, even with those more sober-minded, is there absolute safety under such conditions. However serviceable the vine, clinging to its trellis and maturing its juicy products, let it be displaced by rude and violent hands, and its support be snatched away, — its tendrils snap or are crushed, its form is dishevelled and deflowered, and its glory departs. So, with much of the pious element in a nation. Nothing is more delicate, as a task, than the disentanglement of reverent hearts from false ideals. It demands a trial. The truth of the Almighty is powerful and will assert itself in the presence of superstitions, but who is able for the duty of that gentle, holy transfer by which hearts wedded to base ideas and vain forms shall, while they experience release from the past, feel firmly fastened to better things, and hence more capable of fulfilling the soul's highest expectations?

Disaffections in society call for brief notice as bearing upon the promotion of free thought. In the development of a nation's energies, there will necessarily be those divergencies born of disparity between intellects. All persons do not go out on parallel lines, nor do they reach the same goal, at the same time, or by the same route. In the nature of things this is impossible. Consequently, deep discontents are bred. Whatever the inequalities in gifts or energies, it is required by some, that there shall be equality of results and rewards. This demand is no doubt encouraged by the wrongs, heaped by the wealthy on the heads of the helpless. Financial oppressions beget chafings and disturbance, and the more so where they have their seat in corporations making some pretence to right dealings. Opulent endowment of churches, or aristocratic elements within church walls, grate harshly on the souls of those struggling for a bare existence. Perhaps nothing will quicker turn one from the comforts of a living faith to a morose and melancholy skepticism, than the jealousy engendered by superciliousness of conduct on the part of those more highly favored than ourselves. For the spectator, also, this is productive of bad impressions. By an untoward habit of the mind, God is unrighteously associated with these evils to such an extent as to attach blame to the Divine management. Out of this, anarchy and rebellion burst forth. Reckless men, neither fearing God, nor regarding their fellows, concoct plans for the abolition of the Bible, the destruction of the church, and the disintegration of society. No respect is paid to private property. Physical and moral spoliation is their delight. Communism is their religion, might their law, and self their deity. They set fire to materials that have long since been laid, ready for kindling, by those whose course it is to revel in the luxuries filched, piece by piece, from the laboring classes, dancing and chuckling like fiends of hell around the conflagration. And because of the possibility to trace the origin of much of it into religious quarters, therefore many people who hesitate to give expression to their views in this iconoclastic way, at least divide their sympathies so as to allow the least portion to go in favor of the truth.

We come, now, to the contemplation of some religious causes of free thought. Among the political causes enumerated are seen some traces of this; but, it will be observed, that this was unavoidable by reason of the complications in all national religions. There, consideration was given chiefly to causes originating in the govermnent of people under existing laws. We propose now to examine into the spirit of the religion itself — what it was, and is, and how it has been employed for the production of free thought. In so doing we shall consider jealousies as respects secular knowledge, intolerance of creeds, and corruptions of doctrine and life. That in past times the church has been exceedingly assumptive, — intruding into realms of knowledge belonging to others, — cannot honestly be questioned. Its apology was founded in the fact that it was the professed guardian of secular thought. Its reach was all but universal, embracing philosophies, literatures and sciences, whether physical, social or moral. Nor is it entirely free, as yet, from the aspiration for such dominion. It is not settled with all what is the domain of Christianity. Whether its province is that of foster-mother to every species of knowledge, awarding it sanction, or administering necessary corrections, seems still in debate. While this state of affairs exists we may expect dispute. On the part of scientists, recently there has been great hope that the lines would so be drawn, and religious and secular prerogatives so adjusted, as that collisions would be debarred and jealousies cease. The distinction between the realms of the known and unknown — the visible and invisible — was never more clearly made than now. And were it nor for the fact that even the foremost leaders of scientific thought lose patience at times, bounding beyond the limits assigned by themselves, and speculating as respects the things of God, it is highly probable that Christian thinkers would cheerfully relinquish to them the whole territory of worldly wisdom. Many, as it is, are becoming, daily more thoroughly impressed with the feeling that Christianity is a system of itself, needing no aid from without, and commanding the loftiest attention when it concerns itself with its own momentous affairs. A consciousness is taking possession of us, that a vital, loving diffusion of gospel truth throughout men and nations, their thought and life, is more in keeping with the spirit of Christ than that arrogance that ends in dictatorship; and if Christian people shall be so fortunate as to take the lead in this temper of the mind, it will only be in harmony with these superior principles, which they shall thus be entitled to claim as their own. Having said this much it will scarcely be necessary for us to busy ourselves in dragging up the past or citing such instances as that of Galileo, to show the church's inconsiderate zeal or to condemn her false jurisdiction. Those were days when almost all men and modes of thought were alike persecutors and persecuted. The spirit of rigor was not confined to the church; it belonged to the age.

Perhaps nothing, on the part of religion, has done more to drive thought astray, and into forbidden paths, than the attempt to confine it within theological bounds. Upon the consideration of recondite questions, — such as the trinity or the foreknowledge of God, — the mind delights to revel or delve. Quick and imperfect conclusions, summarized in creeds as adjustments of truth, fret the inquisitive mind and incline it to rebel. The feeling becomes prevalent that the thoughts of God are larger than these limitations allow. Indulging this, and still pained by the restraint it is but just ridded of, the mind flies off at a tangent, seeking an orbit of its own. Much of this rash behavior, however, depends upon the pressure made upon it. The mere fact of the creed's existence cuts no particular figure. Like many defunct laws, it may be buried in the limbo of forgetfulness. Men grow, whether their creeds do or not, and hence the disproportions arising between them forbid active service. That church or people is **indeed unfortunate who, failing to note this necessitous** fact, spends its life in the sorry attempt of shortening in manhood to the limits of that which has long since become obsolete. Here the glorious spirit of liberty rightly asserts itself. Men must have freedom to breathe, and they do not obtain this when corked up in ecclesiastical bottles. Observing this, the most determinate religionists are adopting a more liberal policy towards their devotees. The spirituality of the times proves too strong for them. The barriers they would impose are swept away before the onflowing tide of a better evangelism. Missionaries for Christ are sweeping over the globe, calling men to the Cross, and impressing upon church dignitaries everywhere the need of enforcing upon human attention the graces of a godly life. The bleak and wintry sides of theology are being melted down by the love of God shed abroad in the heart. Fortifications hitherto impregnable (like the massive masonry reared sometime past on our sea-coasts, but futile to stay the entrance of our modern monitors) are compelled to succumb before the approaches of the Gospel.

Really, the serious question now is not how shall we rid the creed of its intolerance, but shall there be any creed at all, or shall the church satisfy itself in a mere emotionism? This change of base is brought about by the crude imitations and base counterfeits of very good and yet very imperfect men. Good, because, loving God and man, they had not had the courage to break loose from ecclesiastical yokes; imperfect, in that they fail to grasp the full conception of God's gospel. Far in advance, as to truth, of much that pretends to the correction of sinful souls, they are but the pioneers to a more perfect way. But to return. What does it avail that synods or conferences declare their theological platforms; that Bibles are brought and placed upon pulpits, or that men are called to the worship of God, if so be that the churches bury these human and divine pronunciations beneath such pietic overflows as are described by our modern revivalism? One may well ask, while sitting under the ministrations of many modern pulpiteers, What is to be our final standard? Towards what goal are religious men to think? What is to be the nucleus around which an intelligent, though sinful, world is to be gathered? These are the questions for us now. The mere desertion of creeds, much less the repeated and all too trite mouthings of the name of Christ over the people, will scarce suffice to call men away from infidel ideas back to God. The demand, we think, is for a substantial faith, — one, that while it shall reach and satisfy the understanding, shall conquer the heart. This, we take it, will be grounded on Christ's everlasting gospel, embracing its facts, doctrine, conditions, duties and hopes, for here alone is wholesome and sufficient food for body, soul and spirit.

In speaking of the corruptions of Christianity as a a cause of free thought, we feel that we are called to note a mighty factor. Degenerate as is the disposition of man, in nothing is he more so, than in his habit of dealing with the system of God. Accommodate Himself as He may to our capacities and wants, man delights in dragging down the truth to his corrupt level.

Perversion and abuse, so liable to the best of things, find their nestling place in the religion of Christ. Rather than to be humbled by the Divine revelation men protect themselves by distorting its primitive grandeur. The light is too pure for·man's eyes without the admixture of darkness. Interlinings and false interpretations are not to be thought of as confined to the speculative or the superstitious, although both these extreme classes indulge largely therein. This is a favorite habit of the immoral. There are more Bibles than the Catholic's that show signs of human fingering; and there are other doctrines than "penance," "indulgence," and "the confessional," that have been elicited therefrom, among all the corruptions of Christianity extant which has not the temerity to assert its Divine origin? To be sure, such is the absurdity of many such claims that they are largely shorn of their power to do harm; and yet when brought to the consideration of the unlettered, supported by such demonstrations as cater to one's superstitions, they frequently acquire a prevailing force.

Nothing is more surprising, perhaps, among the eccentricities of the judgment than the habit of confounding Catholicism with Christianity, so frequently indulged in, not only by lecturing infidels, but also by professed historians. And that the Catholic himself furnishes the authority for it is the more amusing, since it shows the bias of the one, as against Protestantism; while it reveals the want of research on the part of the other. Christianity is a very good thing to lay claim to, without doubt, but verification is first of all in demand. A skeptic, or infidel, may be every way justified in his pronunciation against Catholicism, or, as for that matter, many forms of Protestantism, and yet not touch Christianity by the width of a world. Still all minds do not draw lines thus closely, and, doubtless, much opposition has been made to the gospel by reason of this.

Corruptions in the Christian life is the last cause to mention. Where these abound in vain do the most holy attempt the successful propagation of "the faith." Those who care little or nothing for "The Evidences" take pains to study Christ as he is reproduced in men's lives. By this they measure all the claims made upon them. Unfold whatever of knowledge you may possess respecting God or his revelation, Christ and his salvation, and the joys of an eternal bliss, and it falls as harmlessly as a spent ball upon the ears of him who beholds with his eyes the iniquity of the church. In the stagnant marches of Christian impiety, infidelity is perpetually breeding. Loathe the product as we may it will be well that we do not recognize in it our own offspring. For what reason should *we* build and furnish the armory out of which the weapons are drawn for our own destruction? Or why should we issue from our own spiritual loins a brood of demons to pester and ravage the world?

This concludes our review. It will be seen that it is quite fragmentary. The theme is too vast for full treatment in a brief essay. Only salient points could command attention and they but for a moment. But enough has been said to indicate that in the present imperfect state of man, free thought may find origin, even under the fairest conditions, possible. It is the business of this paper to show how, and to caution its readers so to equip themselves with true knowledge, to use it, and to dispense it, as that minds may be comparatively free from error, and hearts from sin.

DISCUSSION UPON J. W. MONSER'S LECTURE.

A. Proctor said: I am pleased with the breadth of thought exhibited in the lecture. The speaker evidently read up quite widely, and has given us a great deal to think about. There is just one exception I must take to what was said, and that is with reference to what was said concerning a standard of thought. Thought, to be free, cannot be limited by any standard. You cannot put up a goal for yourself, and then think up to it. That is not the way men do any good thinking. The mind must be free to work properly. One of the great benefits of freethinking is in this: that its main quest is for truth without regard to results. Truth is what we all want. There is an authority in truth that asserts itself, and this is sufficient. A man cannot say in advance, here is my standard, and in my investigations my conclusions must be just what I see in this standard. There can be no freedom of thought if he does.

T. P. Haley, inquires whether he understands Bro. Proctor to make no distinction between free thought and freedom of thought? It would seem not, from his last remarks. I undertake to say that a man can enjoy the fullest freedom of thought and yet be in no sense a free thinker, as that term is understood. Here is my friend on my right (refers to a Presbyterian minister) who can, in no true sense, be called a freethinker, and yet I undertake to say he has perfect freedom in the treatment of whatever theme, in whatever method, he may choose. The real thinkers to-day are not free thinkers. The intelligence to-day is in the church, and not among infidels. I should like Bro. Proctor's remarks a great deal better if he would keep this distinction clearly before him.

G. W. Longan: There is no particular difference between free thought and freedom of thought. The free thinkers of the seventeenth century did not mean to convey the idea that infidel thought and free thought is the same thing. The method by which they reached results was what they claimed to be free thought. There was no difference, then, between free thought and freedom of thought. Evidently, the lecturer used free thought to mean infidel thought, and not freedom of thought in the sense that all men are at liberty to think as they please. For years I have been misunderstood on this point. While I think, my brethren, that my heart is wholly loyal to God and to his Christ, I have, and do claim, the right to think as I please, and to express those thoughts as I please, and when I please,

J. W. McGarvey: Bro. Proctor speaks about the authority of truth. I did not know truth had any authority only as it is expressed by persons. If you speak to me about an authority of persons — the prophets, or the apostles, or the Christ — I understand what you mean. But I don't know so well about the authority of truth. Truth, going forth from the lips of a Seneca, or a Socrates, amounted to but little because there was no authority in those who spoke it.

Bro. Longan says he wants the liberty of thinking as he pleases, and of expressing his thoughts as he pleases. I have no objections, so that he will allow others the same privilege. If men take pleasure in propagating heresy, and they will allow the privilege, to the church, of administering discipline when they do this, it will be all right. If we are going to be free, let us be so all around.

C. S. Lucas said: I agree with what Bro. Proctor said; I do not think we can set up any standards to think to. Men do not grow that way. We search for our facts, and form our deductions from them.

J. W. MONSER'S REJOINDER.

I am glad to know that there was so little to except to in my address. Hurried as I was, in its preparation, I felt humiliated at the want of preparation it manifested. The only thing that it seems I am to reply to is this "standard of thought" criticism.

Well! Let us understand each other. I do not question Bro. Lucas' position, that we must search for facts and then form our deductions accordingly. Certainly we must. But what I say is, that we get no valuable results from these deductions until we have chosen some standard of measurement. Am I wild in this remark? Does the geographer, the astronomer, the naturalist, succeed without one? Can you measure the earth, or skies, or behemoth, without one? Will Newton, or Guyot, or Agassiz so attest? Did Darwin amount to much as a scientist until he decided upon the principle of "natural selection?" Until then, was he not roving over the whole earth without a method? Since then, has he not laid everything under contribution to this vast yet simple principle, and has he not built up a gigantic system upon it? Is this not true, also, of Huxley as to "protoplasm," and Spencer as to "evolution?" Does not this last mentioned philosopher write on every department of thought and life with this "standard of measurement" constantly in hand, and can there be any freer thinker than he, take these words in what sense you will?

Now, I maintain that what these philosophers do, we can and should. We can think with the "God" conception, or the "Christ" conception, before us, and do infinitely better thinking than if we allow our minds to ramble about here and there in a very professional, but very pointless way. And even as respects the Bible, I hold that, however conservative and antiquated a man's thought may be, it is vastly better than his who despises the word of God.

VALUE OF METAPHYSICAL STUDY AND ITS RELATION TO RELIGIOUS THOUGHT.

BY O. C. HILL.

THERE are but three possible motives for study: first, to become richer in thought; second, to become stronger in the power of thinking; third, to increase our power and elegance of expression.

The true value of any knowledge or thought depends upon its relation to man's progress and happiness. Many of the ablest thinkers hold that the power acquired in mastering a study is more valuable than the knowledge gained. If this be the case, then metaphysical study must rank very high. There are few studies, if any, that require as close and severe thinking as do metaphysics. There is another method by which we may arrive at the comparative value of metaphysical study. In a broad general sense there are but two things in the universe — matter and force. Matter, in all of its multitudinous forms, is what it is because it has yielded to the forces that are playing through the universe of God. Matter, in any proper sense is not a cause of anything. It does not act, but is acted upon.

A passive agent never can be of as much importance as an active one.

According to Balfour Stewart, there are four planes of physical existence which may be elevated one above another. "They are: (1) The plane of elementary existence; (2) The plane of chemical compounds, or mineral kingdom; (3) The plane of vegetable existence; and, (4) The plane of animal existence." Their relations to one another are truly expressed by writing them one above the other, thus: —

4. Animal kingdom.
3. Vegetable kingdom.
2. Mineral kingdom.
1. Elements.

"Now, it is a remarkable fact that there is a special force whose function it is to raise matter from each plane to the one above, and to execute movements on the latter." Physical force acts on the plane of the elements; chemical affinity, on the plane of the mineral kingdom; vegetable life force, on the plane of the vegetable kingdom, and vital force, on the plane of the animal kingdom. The plane of the elements is a condition for that of the mineral kingdom, the mineral kingdom is a condition for that of the vegetable, and the vegetable, fort hat of the animal kingdom. To make this complete for our present purpose we should place the rational kingdom (in which only man is found) above the animal.

As we go up this arrangement of the material world, we find forms of matter that are higher at each step.

As we examine more closely the lower and higher forms of matter, we find lower and higher forces working upon them. If the form of matter is low, the force is low that produced the form.

Forces that play in the mineral kingdom are lower than those that play in the vegetable, and those that are in the vegetable are lower than those in the animal, and those in the animal, are lower than those in the rational kingdom.

Metaphysics unfolds the laws and explains the operations through which this rational force passes. All of the natural sciences rest upon the first four planes. Chemistry deals with the mineral kingdom, botany, with the vegetable, physiology, with the animal, and metaphysics, with the rational. It is more important to understand the laws of mind than of matter. It is more important to understand the laws underlying the proper development of mind, than it is to understand the laws underlying the formation of crystals.

Mind is a force capable of producing results that elevate and ennoble, or degrade and destroy the individual. No study but metaphysics can deal with the powers and movements of the mind.

If the mind be rightly controlled, a universal song of joy will ascend from every individual heart to the Great Father of us all. The study of metaphysics deals with the highest and most valuable force in the world; in fact, that force to which all others are made subservient; that force for which all others are conditions. In this argument, the value of other studies is not ignored. They are rather the condition of metaphysical study.

We may determine the value of metaphysical study

considered in itself; and, second, as it furnishes the mind with useful knowledge.

The first may be regarded its absolute, and the second, its relative value. In considering the first, we regard man as an end unto himself, and happiness, as the object sought to be obtained by all rational beings. But happiness can only be obtained as man perfects all of his powers. That which is to be the guide in this perfecting process is the mind, and it is patent to all that that which strengthens the guide and gives him the most accurate knowledge concerning himself will be the most useful.

If we regard man as having been created to glorify God, we shall arrive at the same conclusion; namely: that to glorify God most perfectly can only be accomplished by perfecting his powers. Happiness is a result obtained from the right activity of the mind and misery (aside from bodily disease) is a result from a wrong activity of the mind. It would appear from this statement of the case that the primal wisdom of man would be to ascertain exactly what is the right activity of the mind.

But this can be done only as man shall become acquainted with the laws of mind and their mode of operation.

This, however, brings us into the field of metaphysics or philosophy, proper, as Hamilton called it.

When a rational being comes to understand that there are activities in his mind over which he has no more *direct* control than he has over the motions of the planets, then will the importance of metaphysical study begin to dawn upon him. Upon these activities depend his peace, happiness, and solid satisfaction, or his misery, woe, and eternal despair. By a law of the mind there are painted upon the consciousness of every rational being the glories of heaven or the miseries of the damned.

Out of the mysterious depths of human consciousness flow those streams of thought that radiate the soul and become its guide in this wild and turbulent life.

The study of metaphysics is central and should hold a very high place on this ground.

A philosopher said: "There is nothing great on earth but man; in man there is nothing great but mind."

What is of all things the best, asked Chilon of the Oracle. "To know thyself."

Sir Thomas Browne said: "Now, for my life it is a miracle of thirty years, which to relate were not a history, but a piece of poetry, and would sound to common ears like a fable. "For the world I count it not an inn, but an hospital; and a place not to live, but to die in. "The world that I regard is myself; it is the microcosm of my own frame that I cast mine eye on; for the other, I use it but like my globe, and turn it round sometimes, for my recreation.

"Men that look upon my outside, perusing only my condition and fortunes, do err in my altitude; for I am above the shoulders of Atlas."

"The earth is a point not only in respect of the heavens above us, but of that heavenly and celestial part within us. "That mass of flesh that circumscribes me, limits not my mind.

"That surface that tells the heavens it hath an end, cannot persuade me I have any.

"I take my circle to be above three hundred and sixty.

"While I study to find out how I am a microcosm, or little world, I find myself something more than the great. "There is surely a piece of divinity in us; something that was before the elements, and owes no homage to the sun.

"Nature tells me, I am the image of God, as well as Scripture.

"He that understands not thus much hath not his introduction or first lesson, and is yet to begin the alphabet of man."

"Is Truth, or is the Mental Exercises in the pursuit of truth, the superior end."

This is the most important practical problem in the whole range of philosophy. The relative value of various studies in the curriculum of a liberal education will depend upon the way in which we decide this question. Some kinds of truth are much more valuable than others. It is not very important to know the number of the stars and the distances of the fixed stars. To know the number of names of the saints in the calendar is not essential to man's welfare. It is, however, of the utmost importance to have sufficient mental power to successfully fight the battle of life. The failures in life do not depend so much upon a want of knowledge of facts, as it does upon a want of mental power to understand the full import of the facts.

The power to make a steam engine is much more

valuable than to know the names of the different parts of the engine. The ability to paint a beautiful landscape is more important than to know the rules by which the landscape has been painted.

"A truth, once known, falls into comparative insignificance."

Agassiz says: "When a discovery begins to pay, I abandon it, because there are enough inferior minds to take it up when it pays."

"Votaries of science are wilfully ignorant of a thousand established facts — of a thousand which they might make their own more easily than to attempt the discovery even of one."

They do not seek truth *principally*, but the exercise of their powers. Pascal says: "In life, we always believe we are seeking repose, while in reality, all that we ever seek is agitation." We do not play a game of ball for the sake of the knowledge that we get in playing the game, but for the joy in the exercise of our powers in playing. We do not engage in the chase for the sake of the game, but for the delight in the pursuit.

"Man never is, but always to be, blest."

Aristotle says: "The intellect is perfected, not by knowledge, but by exercise." Aquinas says, "The intellect commences in operation, and in operation it ends." "If," says Malebranche, "I held truth captive in my hand, I should open my hand and let it fly, in order that I might again pursue and capture it." The study of metaphysics is one of the best mental gymnastics through which we can pass.

VALUE OF METAPHYSICAL STUDY.

It also comprehends the sublimest objects on which the human mind dwells; the conclusion concerning God, the soul, the present worth and future destiny of man, all are exclusively deduced from the philosophy of the mind. In the science of mind, we can neither receive nor be convinced of anything at second hand. Here each individual must make the discovery for himself. The fact of consciousness, no matter how vividly it may be portrayed to another, or how accurate may be observation, or how able may be the observer, is zero to us until *we* make the discovery for ourselves.

Each student in metaphysics, to all intents and purposes, becomes a discoverer. The hour of supreme delight is the one in which some new truth flashes across our intellectual horizon and opens up to us a field hitherto unexplored.

The value of metaphysical study will be strongly impressed upon us when we attempt to investigate the foundation of human government. All just human governments are founded upon moral law. But moral law is a rule of action for moral beings. There are three things necessary to constitute a moral being; namely: freedom, intelligence, and an end to be chosen.

Without these three elements, no being can be accountable to either human or divine government. Human governments are instituted among men in order to assist them in attaining the end for which they are created. But the object of man's creation cannot be understood without a careful examination of his mental constitution; hence, no thorough understanding of the foundation of human government can be obtained without the aid of metaphysics. Every command to do, or not to do, a specific thing, implies the ability to obey the command.

On any other hypothesis, you would have a command given when it was known it could not be obeyed.

There is nothing more absurd than for one rational being to command another to do that which the latter has no power to do.

It is not only absurd, but positively unjust and wicked, to punish a man for not doing that which he has no power to do. We cannot determine the justice or injustice of punishments without either expressly or impliedly, resting our conclusions upon metaphysics.

Physiology can tell us what the function of the lungs or heart is, but no natural science, however accurate or grand it may be, can tell us why it is right to tell the truth, and wrong to tell a lie.

Man is something vastly different from organized matter. "Man is not an organism; he is an intelligence served by organs."

Both human and divine governments are established to minister to the wants of this intelligence. In fact, everything in the world is subordinate to this intelligence, or man proper; everything revolves around him as a centre; everything was made for his use, but he was not made for the use of any created being: hence, any study that will give us accurate knowledge of this lord of creation is of the highest importance.

Metaphysics is the only study that gives us precise knowledge concerning this intelligence that talks of

VALUE OF METAPHYSICAL STUDY.

heaven and hell, loves and hates, makes war and peace, and, in fact, makes this world a paradise or pandemonium.

It is only through the science of mind that we become acquainted with an order of things vastly different from those presented in the physical world. The law of liberty, of obligation, and the whole field of morals, are revealed through the study of metaphysics. It is only as man is a free intelligence and a moral power that he is created in the image of God.

The meaning of the word *ought* can be explained only by the aid of metaphysics. No rational being feels that he ought to do what he has no power to do. The idea of oughtness does not arise until the individual knows that there is some good in the thing to be done, and that he has the power to do it.

The ideas of merit and demerit can arise only as the mind views its own free operations. The idea of demerit or censure arises in view of the fact, that the mind knows itself to be the author of its own actions; therefore, the idea of condemnation arises whenever our actions are wrong. This idea of censure could not arise if the individual did not know himself to be the author and perpetrator of the wrong action.

Metaphysical study should hold the first rank in the catalogue of studies on account of the intellectual acumen and power developed in a critical study of this science.

It broadens and deepens the conception of the phenomena of psychology. It gives one of the most severe and critical drills in the right use of language.

Without the nicest discrimination in the use of words, no valuable progress can be made in the science of mind. One who uses words loosely can talk for a radiant hour on metaphysics and not say a thing. This is the reason why some people object to the study. But the difficulty is not in the study, but in the weakness of the individual who undertakes to explain the study. By severe labor and an accurate use of terms, this science can be made as plain as a sunbeam.

It throws a flood of light upon a series of subjects, which no other science can touch, of the highest importance to man's welfare and happiness. It throws its refulgent rays upon the foundation of human government; enters the field of morals and brings home to man's consciousness the ideas of right and wrong, and shows how these ideas originate. It enters the very sanctuary of the soul and lays bare the operations of the immortal spirit; shows the exact point of responsibility in thought and action; utters its terrible denunciations and threatenings against every soul that dares to violate the laws of its own being; hurls its awful maledictions against every one who dares to be guided by appetite or desire; and, finally comes as the white-winged dove of peace and joy to all who will give an attentive ear to the low, sweet song that ascends from every soul rightly adjusted to its God and the laws of its own being.

Relation of Metaphysical Study to Religious Thought.

This is a theme that covers almost the entire field of

religion. The relation of metaphysics to religious thought is this: It is the key that solves the difficulties connected with nearly all of the great religious doctrines of the Scriptures. All whose opinions are, at all, valuable recognize three great divisions of the mind, or more properly, three ways in which the mind manifests itself. These divisions are, the Intellect, Sensibility, and Will. The intellect is that power by which we are enabled to know, and, " to know is to be certain of something." It is the office of the intellect to give us certainty on all of those subjects in which certainty can be reached at all.

If certainty ever is reached on any subject, it will be by the operations of the intellect. The sensibility is that through which we enjoy and suffer.

All of our enjoyment and suffering come through the sensibility. The will is that power by which we make choices and decisions.

Take away any one of these divisions of the mind and man would not be a rational, accountable being.

All commands, either human or divine, are directed to the will. This is so, because it is the will that rebels or renders obedience. A clear understanding of the office and products of these three divisions of the mind will enable us to deal rationally with nearly all of the great religious problems. Religion is right feeling and attitude of the will toward God as rightly apprehended. God is a Spirit or mind, and this Spirit can only be apprehended through the laws of mind; hence, metaphysical study is the foundation of all true conceptions of God and His attributes.

God's revelation to the human race was made solely to that part of man's nature of which metaphysics alone takes cognizance. The provisions of this revelation are such that they can be fully complied with on the part of man when they are explained in the light of the laws of mind.

To say that man cannot fully comply with the requirements of revelation is to call in question God's wisdom and goodness.

No being can be either wise or good that requires of those who are under him that which they are unable to perform. To do a thing of that kind would be solemn mockery of man's weakness and helplessness. A wise and benevolent Creator would be more likely to require less, than more than his subjects can do.

Ex-President Finney, of Oberlin College, says: "Every theological system and every theological opinion assumes something as true in psychology.

Theology is, to a great extent, the science of mind in its relations to moral law. " God is mind or spirit; all moral agents are in his image.

Theology is the doctrine of God, comprehending his existence, attributes, relations, character, works, word, government, providential and moral, and, of course, it must embrace the facts of human nature, and the science of moral agency. "All theologians do and must assume the truth of some system of psychology and mental philosophy, and those who exclaim most loudly against it, no less than others."

We cannot take the first step in showing how man can be accountable to any power, either human or divine, without the aid of metaphysics. Man must know himself to be able to obey the behests of law before he can feel himself under obligation to obey.

The word obligation plays a very important part in domestic and religious life. But no rational account can be given of this word without understanding the science of mind. We know that the conditioning ideas of obligation are, a good, intelligence, freedom, and an end.

Without these no man can be under obligation to any being or power. The foundation of obligation is that, in view of which, the idea of obligation is called into being. We are unable to take the first rational step in explaining the fall of man, without resorting to the laws underlying metaphysics. Did the fall consist in a wrong thought, a wrong feeling, a wrong physical act, or a wrong choice? In morals and religion, a choice or decision of the will determines the character of the act. When a man decides to steal, then, that very moment, he becomes a thief in the sight of God, no matter whether he ever steals or not.

When he decides to kill, then, that very moment, he becomes a murderer.

The fall of man consisted in a decision of Adam to disobey a command of God. If Adam had been compelled, by a power superior to his own, to eat the apple, there would have been no fall in the physical act of eating the apple. The commands of God are made to the will of man, because that is *the only* power by which he can make a decision or choice.

Without a decision or consent of the will no act can possess a moral character.

An inspired writer tells us that sin is a transgression of the law.

Do we transgress in thought, or feeling, or a physical act, or choice?

The sin is not in the thought, or feeling, or physical act. It is not in the thought, because we have not direct control over our thoughts. Evil thoughts will come into our minds in spite of our best endeavors to to keep them out. If the sin is in the thought, then, God holds us responsible for doing that which is absolutely beyond our power to do.

The Scriptures teach that we are held for that which we have, and not for that which we have not.

The sin is not in the feeling, because feeling rests upon thought as a basis; therefore, if we cannot think as we please, we cannot feel as we please.

The sin is not in the physical act, because no physical act can have any character whatever, considered apart from the will of the individual who produced the act. Whatever character we ascribe to a physical result, we do so in view of the intentions of the party that produces the result. Two physical acts may be precisely the same, and, one be a sin of the most heinous kind, and the other perfectly sinless. Let two men be shot — the one accidentally and the other intentionally.

The latter (if not done in self-defence) would be murder in the first degree, while the former would be no crime at all. The difference between the two acts is this — a decision, or intention of the will accompanied one ball and not the other. It is true, however, that thought produces feeling, and feeling acts upon the will, but it is within the power of will to decide in favor of the feeling or against it.

No one can give a clear, rational, and scriptural account of faith, that mighty power whose imperial scepter guards ever the entrance to eternal life, that ignores the principles involved in metaphysics. Christian faith has more elements in it than ordinary belief, because James says devils believe and tremble. No one whose opinion is, at all valuable, claims that these imps of darkness have Christian faith.

If they had Christian faith they would not be called devils by an inspired writer. Dr. McCosh says: "Faith is that operation of the soul in which we are convinced of what is not before us. "It is a native energy of the mind quite as much as knowledge is." Dr. Hopkins thus criticises the above definitions: "As related to faith, the operations of the intellect are of two kinds. "They either give us certainty or they do not. "If they give us certainty, that is, knowledge, and not faith. "If they do not give us certainty, then we have belief or opinion, and the reasonableness of the belief, or the value of the opinion will depend on the evidence on which they rest.

"Is, then, our assent to a proposition when there is more evidence for it than against it, Faith?" Certainly not. "If any one is certain, from the operations of his own mind, or in any other way, that there is such a thing as what we may please to call the Infinite, then he knows it as he knows other things. "And if so, let him say so, and not run the whole subject into mysticism by a mysterious principle called Faith, and then opposing faith to knowledge. "Faith, as an energy or principle, can neither be opposed to knowledge nor compared with it, for knowledge is a result. "There is properly no faith till we bring in the element of confidence in a person. "If we believe a thing because a person says so, then there is faith. "Into the confidence we repose in a person there enters an element of choice and of will, which can have no place in any operation of the intellect alone in any of its forms, and without that element there can be nothing that ought to be called faith, or that can be, without introducing confusion."

The important doctrine of the atonement rests for its final solution upon the laws of mental science. It was a scheme introduced by God into his moral government to satisfy public justice and provide a way by which fallen man could return without danger to the moral law. By means of the atonement God was enabled to show his abhorrence of sin and his love for the sinner. It also shows his willingness to make any sacrifice, however great, for the present and future happiness of his wayward children.

Repentance is another one of those fundamental doctrines of the Christian religion that lies at the very foundation of all true Christian character. If there is not a thorough and abiding repentance, no man can enter the kingdom here, or enjoy its blessings hereafter. Does repentance consist in sorrow and remorse for sin? No, this is not that repentance not to be repented of. Sorrow and remorse are only some of the things that are involved in repentance. Paul says: "Now I rejoice, not that you were made sorry, but that you sorrowed to repentance; for godly sorrow worketh repentance to salvation not to be repented of."

This passage teaches that sorrow is only an instrument by which repentance is effected. The instrument by which a thing is done is very different from the thing accomplished.

Repentance is not a phenomenon of intellect or the sensibility. It is a manifestation of the will. It is a change of purpose in consequence of another and more rational view of the subject. Paul says: "Behold what carefulness is wrought in you; yea, what clearing of yourselves; yea, what indignation; yea, what fear; yea, what vehement desire; yea, what zeal; yea, what revenge." If an individual is sorry for his past thoughts and conduct towards God and man, and this sorrow works repentance not to be repented of, evidently he has changed his view and conduct, and this change of conduct can only come through a decision of the will. Anything that is called repentance, and that does not work a change in views and conduct is not repentance at all. "It implies that God is wholly right and the sinner wholly wrong, and a hearty abandonment of all excuses and apologies for sin." Impenitence is something more than a mere absence of repentance. It is an utter refusal to consider the highest interests of God's universe of any importance when compared with the selfish interests of the individual. It is a state of mind wholly at variance with the laws of God and the welfare of man.

It is an utter refusal to be governed by the highest reason that belongs to rational beings.

Justification is a religious question that has involved the Christian world in a good deal of confusion, and the reason of this confusion is to be largely found in a lack of knowledge of those principles underlying all moral government.

What is justification, what its foundation, and what are its conditions? Is justification the pronouncing of one just in view of his own obedience to moral law or in view of Christ's obedience for him? Christ was as much under obligation to render perfect obedience to moral law as any one; therefore, his obedience could not be substituted for that of another. Justification cannot consist in pronouncing one just in view of his own perfect obedience to moral law; because no one has always rendered perfect obedience. "There are none good, no, not one; all have gone astray." Justification is governmentally treating one as just, in view of the atonement and his own obedience to the requirements of the gospel; hence, the atonement and his own obedience are conditions, and not the foundation of justification.

It is a governmental act of amnesty or pardon to those who had incurred the penalty of law.

The ground or moving cause of justification was the infinite love and mercy of God. Before we grasp this subject in its main features we will be compelled to master some of the leading principles of metaphysics.

The next great question that has agitated the religious world is sanctification. There has been much folly connected with this important subject. Some believe in perfect sanctification and others do not.

Perfect sanctification has been defined to be the impossibility of the sanctified to sin They believe it to be a state in which there is no further struggle nor temptation. They say that those who are perfectly sanctified never think evil thoughts. No unhallowed emotions ever reach these sanctified ones in their beatific state. But we know that such an explanation is unphilosophical and unscriptural. In the Scriptures sanctification means set apart to a holy purpose.

The child of God is then set aside for a holy purpose, and this purpose is the well being of man and the glory of God. Is sanctification a phenomenon of the intellect, the sensibility, or the will? It cannot refer to the intellect, because the operations of the intellect considered by themselves are neither sinful nor holy. They have no moral character whatever; therefore, if, by perfect sanctification is meant a state in which the individual is free from evil thoughts, it is an utter impossibility. It cannot refer to the sensibility, because we have no more direct control over it than over the motions of the planets. In the "Outline Study of Man," Dr. Hopkins says: "Through this representative faculty, in connection with other agencies, when once the mind is set in motion, there is a constant succession of thoughts, of feelings, of volitions, passing in a flow as constant as the flow of a river, and as independent of our wills." * * * "The involuntary powers of the mind furnish the material on which its voluntary powers act." The involuntary current brings in thought, feeling, desire. "They come by no will of ours. "A. provokes you, perhaps strikes you; how many impulses, feelings, thoughts, passions, this calls up. "They come of themselves. " You do not will them. "Of the one you say, I accept; and you cherish it. " To the other you say, Down! down! You will have nothing to do with it, and so you control yourself.

"A most blessed thing it would be, would it not, if this part of our nature which is indeed a nature, and nothing else, were never to present to us anything which we should reject, if we could always say to everything thus presented, Yes, yes.

" But it is not thus with any one of us. " It was not always thus with the apostle Paul even. " He could say in view of that which thus presented itself, as well as of the infirmity of purpose in that to which it was presented, Oh! wretched man that I am." If we understand that sanctification pertains to the will, and that perfect sanctification simply means perfect obedience, there will be no difficulty about it.

It is strange that sensible men should believe in perfect sanctification, and then make this perfection to consist in involuntary states of the intellect and sensibility.

There is no involuntary state of the mind, either of thought or feeling, considered independent of the action of the will that is either sinful or holy.

God is love, and this principle is the foundation of the atonement, the scheme of redemption, and all of the benevolent provisions made for man's welfare here

VALUE OF METAPHYSICAL STUDY.

and hereafter. We are commanded to love our enemies. Is the love here commanded synonymous with natural or the moral affections? Must we have the same kind of feelings and emotions for our enemies that we do for relatives and friends, in order to be Christians? If this be required, then Christianity will be a stupenduous failure; because no one can feel the same delight in drunkards, liars, thieves, robbers, and murderers that he does in those who spend their lives in lifting up the fallen and blessing the world by noble deeds of charity and kindness. If we make this love consist in well wishing to our enemies, then the command can be complied with. The love that fulfils the law and the prophets is not a phenomenon of the sensibility, is not an emotion or feeling of any kind; but is choice, a choice to do good to our enemies whenever opportunity presents itself.

Those affections that are natural and nothing more have no moral character. They can neither be praised nor blamed. They are as independent of our wills as the circulation of the blood. It is not so with the moral affections. For these we are responsible. The natural and moral affections blend, and it is not easy to separate them clearly. The moral affections are dependent upon choice for their character. A man may or may not make the love of country supreme. "That depends upon choice." But if he does that, he must have a complacent love for every man into whose face he looks, and who, he knows, has a similar love.

"This is by necessity, but it is in consequence of choice." Had he not made the love of country supreme, this complacent love could not have risen.

"Complacent love and moral indignation may be said to include all the moral affections; the indignation being evolved from the love when the occasion demands it, as its opposite pole. In this love it is that we find the proper ground, and only enduring basis of friendship, as distinguished from mere affinity and combinations on the ground of interest."

The moral emotions, as hope, joy, peace, are dependent upon the moral affections.

The highest emotions of the human soul can only be accounted for upon the principles underlying psychology.

DISCUSSION ON O. C. HILL'S LECTURE.

A. Proctor: I wanted this subject discussed. Materialism is having a great run just now. The leading thinkers of Germany are sending out their thoughts through an English dress, and therefore they come to us and concern us. Bro. Hill has given much thought to the matter in hand, and, I have no doubt, will help to form correct conclusions. I like to see proper distinctions made between matter and spirit.

C. S. Lucas: The region of metaphysical study and the domain of Christian faith are largely the same. The main postulate of Christianity is this: There is an invisible world. Metaphysics means just this, too. Beyond this tangible there is an intangible. Metaphysics means all that is beyond physics — things and thought — the natural and the supernatural. There is no thought without a person. There is a region of things, and a region of persons. All of the visible comes out of, and is a product of the invisible. This building that we are now in was born in the invisible world — that is, in the mind of the architect. The mainspring of Christianity, every enterprise of human endeavor, the principles of faith, hope, and love, all the grand forces which constantly move the universe of God, come out of the realm of the invisible. These intangible, invisible things are the only real things in God's universe, for they are the only things that remain, and that cannot be shaken. "The things that are seen are temporal, but the things which are not seen are eternal." Men are so made as to see the unseen. The eyes of the heart being enlightened go beyond physics into that which is ultimate. It is only as I reach out by the powers of the mind into the beyond that I attain to my truest manhood.

J. W. McGarvey: There is danger in metaphysical study because men become infatuated with it. All that is definite and tangible can be mastered in a little while. I have known men to become infidels by an excessive study of metaphysics. Young men, especially, can be so led on into metaphysics as to have their minds ruined for taking hold of anything practical. Men should be well balanced if they teach youth. Preachers lay themselves liable to danger by studying metaphysics, by bringing such themes to their pulpits.

G. R. Hand: I like this theme. Man to be truly considered must have thought given to his body, soul and spirit. I commend the essay because the lecturer based his thought wisely, and brought it up plane by plane.

J. B. McCleery: I rise to inquire as to whether the terms "mind" and "spirit" are synonymous? Can one take hold of God if He is to be considered immaterial?

O. C. HILL'S REJOINDER.

I am glad, brethren, that there is so little to reply to, and feel myself flattered at the kind reception given to my paper. As respects Bro. McCleery's questions I will say, in a general sense they may be used synonymously, but not, of course, in a specific. An illustration or two will show how I use them. Thought strikes as much as a dagger. If I want to correct my child I do not bathe him, or give him a dose of quinine, but I reason with him, showing him his wrong, and the flush of the countenance indicates the force with which I have reached him. I knew a lady who was killed in fifteen minutes by a thought. The news of the death of a devoted relative struck her heart fatally. Mothers give a practical illustration of the use of metaphysics when one leads her child's mind away from its bad ways by showing it the better way.

Some time since some preachers came to our town who taught the "sanctification" doctrine. Their methods were in a large sense physical and sensational. To those untrained in metaphysics it was difficult to resist the impressions made by the preachers. I found no trouble with my students whom I had taken through a metaphysical course. Once teach young men and women what the laws of the mind are, and you need never fear that "they will be led about by every wind of doctrine."

PREACHERS' METHODS.

J. W. M'GARVEY.

THE duties of preachers are usually well known. They lie on the very surface of the New Testament, and the preacher who does not know them is without excuse. But the best methods of discharging these duties are not so well known. They are not so easily learned, and but few of them are taught in the Scriptures.

There are two ways of learning methods. We learn them by experience and by precept. The latter should precede the former: for experience teaches largely by means of the mistakes which we make, and wise precept preceding experience, if heeded, must save us from many mistakes. But precept, however wise, is seldom accepted in its fulness until we have tested it by our own experience. Experience is the only guide that we are willing to trust implicitly, yet no man should ever consider himself too old or too wise to profit by the experience and the advice of others. The two teachers, experience and precept, should be heard continuously, and every preacher should continue to grow by the help of each until the inevitable decay of old age sets in.

The object of the present lecture is not to dictate, but to advise; not to suggest the only good method as though there were but one, but to state what appears to the speaker the best method of discharging the duties which come under notice. Precepts of this kind are calculated not to better the minds of preachers, but rather to set them free by waking up thought, concerning methods which have been adopted without thought.

It is impossible to satisfactorily discuss, within the space of a single lecture, all the methods included in the subject which I have chosen. These might be distributed in a general way into Methods of Study, Methods of Delivery, Methods of Conducting Public Worship, Methods of Church Work, usually called Pastoral Work, and Methods of Personal Advancement. I will confine my remarks to the first of these and consider the methods, first, of studying the Scriptures, second, of studying other books, third, of making special preparation for the pulpit, and fourth of maintaining system in study.

I.

STUDY OF THE SCRIPTURES.

It is a common thought among the masses of the people that preachers pass their lives in studying the Bible. This appears to be their supreme work, requiring that they be freed from business cares and manual labor. It is doubtless true that they do study the Scriptures more than any other class of men, but no men know so well as preachers themselves, how wofully this duty is neglected. If I were to point out what I believe to be the greatest defect, not call it the greatest sin, in the lives of preachers, I think I would say it is their neglect of the word of God. The common thought of the people just mentioned is that which ought to be. They have a right to demand of every preacher, after he shall have spent some years in his calling, that he be well acquainted with all of God's word, and that he be able to give an intelligent answer to the questions commonly arising on every part. In order to do this it is necessary that he shall have studied the Scriptures laboriously and systematically.

There are four methods of studying the Scriptures, all having their respective advantages and all necessary to the highest attainments. We may study them historically, by books, by topics and devotionally. We will speak of these methods separately and in the order named.

By the historical study of the Scripture we mean the study of its various events and records in the order of time. It aims at obtaining a knowledge of all the events recorded in it, including the composition of its various books, in the order of their occurrence. There are but few books in the Bible in which all the events which it mentions are arranged in chronological order, and there are many which cover the same period of time with other books. In all these instances the facts recorded must not only be known, but we must learn to know them as far as possible in the order of their occurrence. The books of Kings and Chronicles, for example, must be interwoven with one another on the warp of chronology, and all the events recorded as referred to in the contemporary writings of prophets and poets, must be assigned their proper places amid the events of the historical books. In this way alone can we know in full the history of ancient Israel. In like manner, we must not only become acquainted with the four Gospels separately, but we must know the recorded events in the life of Jesus in the order of time if we would understand them; and so of Acts and the Epistles. Those Epistles which are contemporaneous with Acts, fill up in a good degree the historical gaps in that book, while the later Epistles continue the history of the apostolic church beyond the close of Acts.

Such a study of the whole Bible is absolutely necessary to the attainment of general Scripture knowledge. It lies at the very beginning of a course of Scripture study, and it lays the only broad foundation for all subsequent study of Scripture topics. It is by this means alone that the gradual progress of revelation, and the consequent gradual elevation of mankind can be understood; and it may be doubted whether any one important event, or the composition of any one book of the Bible can be properly understood until it is viewed, as this method of study alone enables us to view it in the light of the events and the writings which precede it, and of those which follow it. I would advise every preacher, both old and young, who has never pursued such a course of study, to undertake it at once, and to prosecute it with vigor.

The study of the Bible by books is involved, to a large extent, in the method of study just named, and especially is this true of the historical books. But a man may acquire a good knowledge of events recorded in a historical book without having studied the book as a book — without, in other words, having given attention to the specific design of the book, as to the plan on which it is constructed. No one understands a book until he has done this. And in regard to the books which are not historical, while the student of sacred history may have gleaned the facts mentioned in these, and may have given the book itself and the author of it their proper place in the procession of biblical events, he may as yet have learned very little of what the book contains. When we have gleaned, for example, the historical facts embodied in the book of Job, in the Psalms, in Proverbs, in any of the prophets or in any of the epistles, how much remains that is yet to be learned? How much, too, that is, if possible, of more importance than the facts — matter to which the facts sustain only such a relation as does the scaffold to the building, or the golden framework to the gem which glitters within its embrace. In order to reach and gather this rich fruitage of Bible knowledge, every single book in the Bible must be made, in the course of a preacher's life, a subject of minute and patient study.

The method of studying a single book is simple and obvious. It requires that we first obtain a general conception of its design and its contents. This is obtained by reading it for that special purpose.

This prepares the way for the second step, which is to ascertain the general divisions of the book, together with the aim and contents of each. When this is accomplished the framework of the book, showing the plan on which it is constructed, is distinctly before the mind, and we are prepared for the more minute examination of its particular parts. While reading it for these purposes, we will usually have formed some acquaintance with its historical connections, such as the time and circumstances under which it was written, and the influences at work upon the mind of the author. Next follows an exegetical study of every part by sentences and paragraphs. Much of this information can be obtained by reading an introduction to the book, but this is to obtain information at second hand — a process never to be adopted by a student except when the original sources are beyond his reach. Read introductions after you have studied the books and not before. Thus read, they may correct or modify your own conclusions, but read in advance they may mislead you and at best you are not able to judge of their correctness.

In addition to the study of Bible books separately, many of them should be studied in groups, according to their subject-matter, or the time of their composition. For example, the books containing the scattered statutes of the Mosaic law are a group by themselves; the prophets before the captivity, the prophets of the captivity, and the prophets after the captivity are three other groups. In the New Testament the four Gospels are a group having common subject-matter, and yet John's Gospel, if grouped according to time, would stand with his three epistles and the Apocalypse, as the latest writings of the New Testament. In like manner the apostolic Epistles should be studied in groups according to the time of their composition. Only in this way can we have before our minds the state of society which was before the minds of the writers, and possess the key to the vivid appreciation of these writings which these circumstances alone can furnish.

The study of the Scriptures by topics is the third method which I have named. While prosecuting the methods already mentioned, a general knowledge of leading topics will have been obtained; but the preacher should never be satisfied with a general knowledge of any topic treated in the Bible. Detached pieces of information are never satisfying, and they are very likely to prove misleading. Complete, systematic and exact information is what our calling demands, and this we must as soon as possible acquire.

I know of no method by which such a knowledge of topics can be acquired less laborious than the following: First, by means of your recollection from former readings, and by use of your Concordance, gather up all the passages which treat of the subject in hand, or which throw any light upon it. Second, classify these passages according to the different branches of the subject with which they are connected. The branches of the subject are often known in a general way before the investigation begins. They have come into notice by inquiries of your own mind, or they have been made familiar by religious controversy. When the divisions thus suggested are but a part, the passages themselves will suggest the remainder, so that there will seldom appear any difficulty in completely classifying the collected passages and obtaining exhaustive subdivisions of the topic. The next step is to arrange the thoughts and facts under each branch of the subject in some natural order of sequence, and thus obtain a systematic view of it as it stands in the Scriptures. Finally, the parts must be studied with reference to one another and the whole; and the whole must be studied with reference to all its parts. When this is done you are prepared, and not till then, to write or speak on the subject or any of its parts with the assurance of one who understands fully what he proposes to say.

This is a laborious process. It is one which only the few have the industry to pursue; but the few who do pursue it are the masters in Israel, they are the teachers of teachers; while those who lack this industry must remain contented with very imperfect knowledge, and must obtain their knowledge in the main at second-hand. I suppose myself to be addressing men who wish to rank with the former of these two classes. It may be well to add, however, that a young preacher, in the beginning of his ministry must necessarily discuss some subject before he can have had time and opportunity for this exhaustive study; but all such should remember that this necessity is one of the disabilities of inexperience which must be put away as soon as possible.

In the last place, I am to speak of studying the Scriptures devotionally. The preacher who has not a devotional spirit, lacks the chief elements of power with the people both in the pulpit and out of it. He is utterly incapable of cultivating a devotional spirit in his hearers; and without this the entire service of the church becomes an empty form. No man who is to lead the people in the way of life can afford to neglect this element of the Christian character, this source of religious enjoyment, this element of pulpit power. Apart from frequent prayer and much meditation, there is no way to cultivate this spirit except by the thoughtful reading of those portions of Scripture which are especially designed to awaken devotional sentiments. The preacher, therefore, should study these portions a great deal. They should be in his hand every day.

When we speak of devotional parts of the Scriptures, the mind turns at once to the book of Psalms; for in it are collected the richest poetic effusions of pious hearts throughout the period of Jewish inspiration, from Moses to the poets of Babylonian captivity. But only a certain portion of these is well adapted to the cultivation of devotion. Some of them are descriptive, some didactic, and a few are vindictive, giving utterance to that sentiment of the Mosaic law which allowed the demand of an eye for an eye and a tooth for a tooth. By frequent reading of all the Psalms, the preacher will make himself acquainted with those which contain pure devotional feeling according to the Christian standard, and these should be his sources of inspiration.

But besides the Psalms, there are many passages in Job, in Ecclesiastes, in Proverbs, in the prophets, and even in the historical books of the Old Testament, the study of which lifts up the soul to the loftiest sentiments, while in the New Testament, which contains not a single book of poetry, there are passages in the Gospel, in Acts, in the Epistles, and in the Apocalypse, fully equal to the sublimest poetry for filling the soul with every holy emotion. The preacher, while studying the Scriptures historically, by books and by topics, will have found all these passages. He should mark them as he discovers them, and should subsequently revert to them, for devotional reading until both their contents and their places in the book became familiar to him.

In order to the best effect upon our hearts, our devotional study should not consist in a mere dreamy reading of the parts referred to; for in this way the impression made is likely to be shallow and transitory. We should study these passages exegetically, searching into the significance of every figure employed, and trying to paint before imagination's eye every image projected by the writer. If we read, "The Lord is my shepherd, I shall not want," we do not feel full force of the metaphor until we learn all about the work of a Palestine shepherd, as it is alluded to throughout this Psalm, and as it is literally described by Jesus in the tenth chapter of John. So of all the metaphors, tropes and historical allusions throughout the poetry of the Bible.

But the best effects of devotional study will still lie beyond our reach, if we do not commit many of these inspiring passages to memory, so that we can meditate upon them in the night watches, call them up amid our labors and our journeyings, and make them subjects of conversation when the Bible is not at hand. It is in this way that the word of God is to dwell in us richly in all wisdom. If you will inquire you will find it almost universally true of men and women eminent for piety, that their memories were vast storehouses for the most precious portions of God's Holy Book.

As a kind of concluding note I must append to this part of my lecture the remark, that in all of our study of the Scriptures we must constantly consult the original if we can, and that we must by all means use the best version. The Canterbury revision of the New Testament should now totally supplant the King James version, not only because it is a great improvement as a version, but because it is the only representative in English of the corrected Greek text. A man is not safe in venturing upon the exegesis of a single passage by the aid of the old version until he shall have compared it carefully with the new; and rather than be continually making these comparisons, it is better to at once adopt the new into exclusive use.

II.

STUDY OF OTHER BOOKS.

From this brief treatment of the study of the Scriptures, we pass to the study of other books, and first to the study of Commentaries. This is really but another method of studying the Scriptures, yet it may properly received separate treatment.

There is a well known prejudice against the use of Commentaries, but it is confined to a small and decreasing number of persons. The man who attempts to gain a knowledge of the Bible by his own unaided powers, while the aid furnished by a multitude of learned and devout predecessors is at hand, seems to declare himself the equal in exegetical power of all have who gone before him. In no other department of human study do we reject the aid of our fellow-students; why should we reject it in this?

Good Commentaries render us important service in many ways. First they serve as a guard against blunders. Among the most egregious blunders in the interpretation of Scripture are those committed by men of inferior learning or judgment who interpret the Scriptures without aid. The use of a judicious Commentary guards us against many blunders of this kind, and it corrects many a mistake into which we fall before the Commentary is consulted. In the second place, it is a ready source of information. Multitudes of facts and references throwing floods of light upon important passages have been collected by the research of commentators, and furnished to our hand, which would otherwise be beyond our reach, or, if we reach them at all, it would be after years of toil and the reading of thousands of pages. No man can afford to decline the use of these gathered treasures. True it would strengthen his powers to gather them for himself, but he may strengthen his powers much more rapidly by gathering up these, and then by the aid of these, going out to search for others. The speculator who wishes to make millions never rejects the few thousands already within his grasp, but he uses the thousands as the means of getting the millions. In the third place, the use of Commentaries awakens thought. Every one that is worth consulting presents the subject in some new phase; it presents something different from and often inconsistent with our own previously formed conceptions; and it compels us to think again over the whole ground. Such recasting of thought on a subject is necessary to intelligent confidence in our final conclusions. In the last place, Commentaries, with all the errors which may be properly charged against them, do in the main give us the right interpretation of obscure passages, and the right application of those which are not abscure. If we follow them implicitly we are but seldom led astray, and if we find in them only a confirmation of our own conclusions this gives us strength and gratification.

While I insist, however, upon the value of Commentaries, I would also insist upon a judicious use of them. When about to study a passage of Scripture, never consult the Commentary first. If you do you are likely to accept the author's views, whether right or wrong, and your mind will be biased in the subsequent study of the text itself. First study the text until its words and sentences are distinctly apprehended; until all that is clear in it is understood; until its difficulties are discovered; and until your own mind has grappled with these difficulties more or less successfully. You are then prepared to consult the Commentary. As you read it you know of what it treats; you can judge of the correctness of its statements; you can see where it touches the difficulties; and you can accept or reject the explanations which it gives with an intelligent judgment.

I would suggest as another precaution in regard to Commentaries, that the young preacher take pains, as soon as practicable, to procure two or more on every portion of Scripture which he studies, lest he become a blind follower of a single guide, who, in some places, is almost certain to be a blind guide. In making selections, always choose from the more recent rather than from the older works. In all departments of literature immense advances are being made on the knowledge and methods of former times, and in no department are they more rapid than in the interpretation and illustration of the Bible.

The best commentaries in English on the whole Bible are Lange's, and the Bible Commentary, sometimes called the Speaker's Commentary, because the preparation of it was first proposed by the Speaker of the House of Commons. Commentaries on the New Testament, and on special portions of it, are very numerous, and many of them are excellent; but Ellicott's works contain the finest specimens of grammatical exegesis, and Lightfoot's the finest in the way of profound historical research.

There are some other Biblical works, the study of which is scarcely less important than that of Commentaries. Of these I will mention a few, and foremost among them all, Smith's Bible Dictionary. This great work might be regarded as a commentary on the whole Bible arranged in the order of subjects and not in that of books, chapters, and verses. It contains the cream of all the knowledge possessed by the most cultivated minds in Great Britain, on all Bible themes, including all places and persons mentioned therein. Only in the geography of Palestine, I believe, have more recent investigations superseded it in important particulars.

Next to this in value I would place the Life and Epistles of Paul, by Conybeare & Howson. It is scarcely saying too much of this work to assert that to the man who has not studied it, it offers a new revelation on Acts of Apostles and the Epistles of Paul. As a companion to the Old Testament, Rawlinson's History of the Seven Ancient Monarchies is of almost equal value. It supersedes all other ancient histories, and makes full use of the historical materials derived from the disinterred libraries of the ancient world. There has recently appeared in English a series of works covering in part the same ground with the Life and Epistles of Paul just mentioned, but reaching backward and forward of it in point of time, with which every preacher should become familiar. The Life of Jesus, by Strauss, followed by Bauer's Life of Paul, and his Church History of the first three centuries, and these followed in France by the Jesus, the Paul, and the Apostles, of Ernest Renan, opened a new era in infidel literature, one in which a large number of eminent men have undertaken the entire reconstruction of New Testament history, with all that is miraculous left out. These efforts have called forth two works in France, now found in an English dress, and three in Great Britain, which are among the best of all modern contributions to Biblical literature. They are Pressense's Life of Jesus, and his Early Years of Christianity; and Canon Farrar's Life of Jesus, His Life and Epistles of Paul, and his Early Days of Christianity. These works, without taking the form of direct replies to the works of Strauss, Bauer, and Renan, are written from the new point of view suggested by those works, and they contain a complete vindication of the historical truthfulness of the New Testament. I sincerely regret, in regard to the profound and eloquent works of Canon Farrar, that I am constrained to modify my commendation of them by cautioning the reader against his belief in a *post mortem* gospel, and his inadequate conceptions of inspiration.

In addition to Biblical works of the kind just mentioned, the preacher should also study works on the Evidences of Christianity. It is no reproach to a man of little education and poor opportunities for study, that he believes in the divine authority of the Bible, not because he has made a special study of its evidences, but because he has been educated to this belief. The value of faith is determined, not by the source whence it is obtained, but by the effect which it has on our lives. Of the preacher, however, more than to his is rightly expected. He should know for his own sake, and in order that he may teach it to others and defend it when attacked, the line of evidence which supports our faith.

The exhaustive study of evidences is a lifetime work. The books on the subject are numbered by the hundred. Some of the questions involved are exceedingly intricate, requiring much learning and research for their solution; new questions are constantly arising, and the line of defence, as a consequence, is ever changing. Only the few who are possessed of learning, leisure, and libraries, can explore the entire field. But there is, and from the nature of the case there must be, a fixed line of positive evidence on which the faith has always rested, and on which it must continue to rest to the end of time. With this every preacher should endeavor to make himself familiar; and he will find that, in the main, it is simple and very direct.

It is better, when practicable, to begin the investigation of questions in dispute with some fact admitted by all ,parties, so that all may start from common ground. This rule would suggest as the very first question in a course of study in Evidences, the inquiry whether the Greek and Hebrew Scriptures, which we now have in hand, as all parties to the controversy know, have been so preserved from the date of their composition as to be substantially the same that they were originally. If it cannot be made to appear that they are, the investigation need not go any farther; for what is the use of spending time to prove the divine origin of an ancient book if no reliable copy of it has been preserved to us? The study, then, of the state of the Greek and Hebrew text, by the aid of works on Biblical Criticism, is the first task before the student of Evidences. But though first in logical order, it is the last in the order of actual development. Biblical Criticism cannot yet be called a completed science; for, while it has almost completed its task on the New Testament, it has done comparatively little on the Old. Still, enough has been done to assure the student that in the whole New Testament, with well defined exceptions of brief passages and single words on which we can place our fingers, we have the very words and syllables which were penned by the inspired writers. The number of those yet doubtful is rapidly diminishing under the hands of the critics, and none of them leaves doubtful any matter of doctrine or duty. The best works to study on this subject, taken in the order in which I name them, are the History of the Printed Text by Tregelles, Scrivener's Introduction to the Critical Study of the New Testament, and the Appendix to Westcott & Hort's edition of the Greek Testament.

Having satisfied ourselves that the New Testament books have come down to us without material change, we must next inquire when and by whom these books were written. Were they written by the authors to whom they are commonly accredited, or are they spurious compositions of a later date? It is idle to inquire into the inspiration of the authors until we know who the authors were. On this subject, commonly known under the title of the Canon of the New Testament, the preacher will find much valuable information in the introductions to the various books in his Commentaries, and he will find similar information in his Bible Dictionary. After mastering these he is prepared to study appreciatively Westcott's work on the Canon, the most masterly work on the subject now extant in the English language. He will find, also, nearer home, in Prof. Fisher's Supernatural Origin of the Bible, and Ezra Abbott's small work on the Genuineness of the Gospel of John, some special arguments of very great value.

Having traced the New Testament books to their reputed authors, we next inquire what evidence these books furnish, apart from their claim to inspiration, in favor of the divinity of Christ. This depends upon their authenticity. If their statements in matters of fact are reliable, including what they say of the miraculous, then, whatever may be the qualifications of the writers in other particulars, the claims of our Redeemer are established, and the Christian religion is proved to be of divine origin and authority. This question is treated here and there, in connection with particular passages, throughout all the good Commentaries, and there are several most excellent works devoted entirely to its discussion. Of these I may mention, as among the most valuable, Blunt's Coincidences, Paley's Horae Paulinae, and Rawlinson's Historical Evidences.

But when we have proved that Jesus is the Christ, the Son of the Living God, our task is not yet completed. However true the claims of Jesus, and however truly and authoritatively he spoke, unless we have a reliable account of his teaching, we know not how to avail ourselves of the blessings which it offered to the world. Moreover, a very large part of the teaching found in the New Testament came not from him, but from the pens of his disciples, and unless they possessed some qualification for speaking with authority in matters spiritual and eternal, we are thrown back at last upon our own fallible judgment to decide what is right and true. This makes it necessary that we next inquire whether or not these writers were inspired, and to what extent their inspiration guarded them against error. If when writing they were miraculously inspired of God, then all that they have written is infallibly true; if not, then every man is left to judge for himself when they speak the truth and when they do not.

While almost any work on the general subject of evidences that you may take up, and every valuable Commentary, contains proofs of the inspiration of New Testament writers, and while inspiration of some kind is conceded to them even by many extreme rationalists, I am not able to name a work which, in my judgment, contains a thoroughly satisfactory discussion of the nature and extent of inspiration. It is purely a Biblical question, to be determined by statements of the Scriptures themselves. As a brief outline of a course of study on the subject, I recommend that we inquire first of all, what Jesus promised his disciples in the way of inspiration. Examine these promises with the utmost care, so as to determine with the greatest possible precision what they mean. Secondly, let us examine with equal care what the Apostles claim to have realized in fulfilment of these promises. Thirdly, consider the bearing of all facts recorded which tend in any way to modify the promises and the statements concerning their fulfilment, and let these have due weight in forming our final conclusions. In this way alone, it seems to me, can an adequate theory of inspiration be evolved, and in this way every man of fair scholarship and sound judgment can safely prosecute the inquiry. I commend it to my brethren in the ministry as one of the most important inquiries which can in this age engage their attention. There is no other question on which the minds of preachers are now more unsettled, and there is none on which it is more important that we have settled convictions. If a man fall into doubt concerning the inspiration of the sacred writers, though his faith may appear to live, it is dead — it is rotten at the core.

At the close of this series of inquiries, the student of evidences is ready to gather up and appreciate a multitude of collateral and of independent arguments which are scattered through the books on the subject, and he is also ready to enter upon the consideration of all objections and of all arguments on the other side which he shall not have encountered already. In regard to the latter, I have a suggestion to submit, which may be dignified by the title of a rule to govern our readings in evidences. Never read an attack on the Bible at a given point until the Bible at the point of attack is understood, and its evidences known. Of course, you may stumble upon some attack, or you may look into a work, or listen to a lecture, for the purpose of ascertaining what attack is made. But when a book is within your reach which you know contains an attack on a particular part of the Bible or on a particular line of its evidence, never read that book until you have made yourself acquainted with that which it attacks. This is but a maxim of common sense, and its observance is necessary to fairness. It is enforced in courts of justice and in all properly conducted discussions. The evidence which the plaintiff can furnish in support of his claims is always heard before that of the defendant who attacks his claim; and in criminal cases, the only reason why the accuser is heard first, is because he claims that a crime has been committed by the defendant, and the evidence in support of his claim must be first heard. In public discussions, no one hears the negative until after he has heard the affirmative. If you listen to unfriendly representations of a person before you are acquainted with him, you may be prejudiced against one whom you would otherwise highly esteem; and if you hear unfavorable statements concerning a book which you have never read, you can scarcely do justice to it when you read it. So it is with the Bible. Thousands of unbelievers owe their unbelief to the fact that they have listened to the negative in the discussion concerning its claims, before they have heard and understood the affirmative. No grosser injustice could they have perpetrated against their own minds or the Bible.

Before leaving this general division of my subject, I must add a suggestion in regard to the reading of general literature. It has been truly said that there is no department of knowledge which the preacher cannot make subservient to his high calling; yet there is a limit to the possibilities of acquisition, and he who limits his efforts at acquisition to that which will do him the best service is the one who studies most wisely. As a rule, an earnest preacher's knowledge of general literature is confined chiefly to what he acquires before he enters fully upon his life work; for after this, literature belonging to his special department is so urgent in its demands and so enormous in quantity, that if he does it justice it will absorb all of his time. Still, there are hours of relaxation in which a brief excursion into neighboring fields is refreshing to the student and from it he will usually bring back some valuable spoils.

III.

SPECIAL PREPARATION FOR THE PULPIT.

On the subject of special preparation I must speak very briefly. As I could not cover the entire ground without giving a synopsis of some work on Homiletics, I will only attempt a few suggestions on points which need, I think, to be emphasized.

First of all, I ask, what is the *purpose* of a sermon? Its structure, the material which enters into it, and the special study which precedes it, will all be determined by its purpose. It is feared that some sermons are prepared and delivered for the purpose of making a reputation. In all such the apostolic rule is reversed, and the preacher preaches himself, not the Lord Jesus. Other sermons have in view, as their chief aim, the improvement of the preacher as a public speaker. This also is a selfish end, and a prostitution of the noblest office ever committed by God to man. A better class of sermons are intended merely to impart instruction. These, while aimed in the right direction, fall short of the proper aim of a sermon. This aim, if we judge by all of the apostolic sermons, and by all that is said in the New Testament about preaching, is to bring about some change for the better in the life of the hearer. To this end instruction is but tributary, and for this reason it holds a subordinate place. No sermon is effective without instruction, nor is it effective without exhortation. We teach that we may have a basis for exhortation, and we exhort that we may move to proper action. The last is the supreme purpose to which all else is to be carefully subordinated.

If this view is correct, then the very first step in the special preparation of a sermon, is to select the special change for the better at which it shall aim. This determined, the subject is determined, and often the passage of Scripture which contains the subject. Sometimes, it is true, a certain subject suggests a certain end to be attained by a sermon, and often a passage of Scripture on which the mind is dwelling suggests the subject of a sermon and its aim. But in these cases it is still the practical aim in view which settles the mind upon the choice of that particular passage and that particular subject.

When the special aim of the sermon has been fixed, and the subject or the particular Scripture passage to be employed has been selected, the next step is to study the selected passage until the author's real thought is ascertained. This and this only should be presented as the teaching of the passage. To wrest the word of God for an evil purpose is one of the greatest of sins. To wrest it for a good purpose, though not so bad, is still a sin, and it is a sin quite common in the pulpit. It is to do evil that good may come. It is deceptive, because it has the appearance of doing what is not done, and it leaves on the minds of many hearers a permanent misconception of the passage which is misconstrued. If a text properly construed, whether it be your principal text, or others employed in the progress of the sermon, does not serve your purpose, find others that do, and if you can find none that do, then conclude either that your purpose is unscriptural, or that you are not yet sufficiently acquainted with the Bible to speak with that purpose in view.

It is also highly important that when the preacher has selected his subject, he make himself thoroughly acquainted with it before speaking on it. Otherwise he is in danger of taking positions which fuller information would require him to modify or abandon. Multitudes of the blunders and errors which are constantly disfiguring pulpit efforts and which often make them sources of greater evil than good, result from neglecting this rule. The rule requires us to gather before us all the passages of Scripture which treat of the special subject in hand, to study every one with reference to the particular light which it throws upon the whole subject, and when we have made our selection to treat it in the light shed upon it by all the other passages. The careful observance of this rule will save the preacher from many a blunder and will prove to him a very fruitful source of rich and solid material out of which to construct subsequent sermons.

There are two parts of the sermon always requiring very careful attention, which are very commonly neglected. I mean the introduction and the conclusion. A good introduction, fixing the attention and winning the favor of an audience, gives the preacher a vantage ground at the outset and wins half the battle before the real struggle begins. It should never be left to the spur of the moment, but it should be carefully studied as an outgrowth of the sermon; for though, like a preface to a book, it comes first to others it often comes last to yourself.

Good introductions are more common than good conclusions. How often we have heard sermons which moved on steadily and impressively until near the close, and then struggled as if sinking in the mire. We could see just how far the preacher had made careful preparation, and as soon as he passed that limit we could see that he began to flounder. Perhaps we have been that preacher (who of us has not?) and can remember how we beat about for a landing place and could not find it, — how we felt every moment that our sermon was being whittled down to the little end of nothing, though we struggled with might and main to give it a better ending. All this is the result of defective preparation. We stopped preparing before we got through and as a consequence we got through the sermon before we quit speaking. To avoid this disaster, which sometimes sends a man home, feeling as if he never had preached well and never could, we must be careful to fix upon a conclusion and to prepare it thoroughly.

This should be done also for two other reasons. First, it is the beginning and the end of the sermon which are most distinctly remembered by the average hearer. When he has forgotten everything else that was said, he remembers these. Second, it gives greater power and ease to the preacher himself all through the sermon. His conclusion, if a good one, contains in the concentrated form of earnest appeal, the practical aim of the entire discourse. Everything he says is aimed at it, and he approaches it at every step. He knows his landing place and he feels increasing strength as he advances toward it. It animates him from the beginning and it lifts him high when he reaches it. His hearers must be hard of heart if he does not lift them with him.

In all that I have said on the subject of special preparation, I refer to preparation for preaching, not for writing. If a man, after thus preparing to preach a sermon concludes to commit it to writing, either before or after delivering it, he does well, provided he does so not for the purpose of reading it to an audience, or of printing it, or of committing it to memory and reciting it. There is a great difference between preaching and reciting a memorized sermon. The former is a living thing, the latter is a machine. There is a still greater difference between preaching and reading a sermon. When the reading is real reading, as when one reads a book, it is a tame affair in the pulpit. When it is not real reading, but a kind of make-believe in which the speaker half reads, half recites and tries to convince the audience by gesticulating and posturing, and hiding his manuscript, that he is preaching, the performance is a farce, and the people would laugh it out of countenance were it not for the solemn service with which it is connected.

IV.

SYSTEM IN STUDY.

There are some preachers who read a great deal and do some studying, but never reach proportionate attainments because of a want of system. There are many others, who for the same reason never find time for much reading or study, and who consequently make but little growth. The only way to accomplish much in this bustling and distracting world, whatever be our line of work, is to work in a systematic way — to have a time for everything, and to do everything in its time.

Preachers who are moving about from church to church, and from house to house engaged in protracted meetings or missionary work, are apt to imagine that they have no time for study. But it is entirely practicable for them to spend some hours almost every day at a particular time of day in hard study, if they will. It requires only a little resolution and a polite apology to the friends who would otherwise expect your company, and who would perhaps be glad at times to be rid of entertaining you.

System in study requires much more than the mere appropriation of regular hours to study. It requires the steady prosecution of selected lines of study, and the proper distribution of our time between these. It is not well to give our whole time for any considerable period to one line of study; nor must we divide it between too many. The study of the Scriptures should occupy a fixed part of every day. If one devotes but a single hour every day to the study of the Scriptures historically, or by books, or topically, and shall compute how much this will amount to in a year, he will be astonished at the result. In the course of a lifetime it would make him intimately acquainted with every part of the Bible. And besides the study for mere knowledge, he should give another part of every day to devotional study. Should a man take time to only commit to memory a single verse of a Psalm and meditate upon it every day, in the course of a year he would commit at least twenty Psalms, and he would have all of them in about seven years. I mention these small figures, not because a preacher should be content with them, but to show by the results of a little systematic study that more can be accomplished than those who lack system are apt to imagine.

As preaching is the preacher's business, the special study of sermons should of course occupy just so much of his time as is necessary to the very best preaching of which he is capable. It cannot occupy all of his time, because the general lines of study which we have marked out are necessary for the accumulation of material on which to expend the special study of sermons; but the most pressing demand upon the preacher's time, and the demand which must at all hazards be met, is that which is made by the preparation of sermons.

Give me a man of ordinary talents and earnest piety, who steadily and perseveringly through life pursues such a system of study as I have marked out, and I will show you a preacher who will always be sought after by churches that have him not; who will never leave a community except against its protest; who will count his converts by the thousands, if he live long; who will count in still larger numbers the struggling souls whom he shall have helped on their heavenward way, and who will finally bring an abundance of sheaves into the eternal granary.

DISCUSSION ON J. W. M'GARVEY'S LECTURES.

A Proctor: I have no reflections to pass on the lecturer. I have known him for years as a studious, painstaking man, and he has shown it to-day by the amount of good advice he has gathered together in these lectures. As for myself, I had not the opportunity in my young days to profit by such information. I seem to be an exception to all rules, and yet I am no example to the younger preachers. I have too many defects. I find, however, that I can get my sermons best by keeping near to Christ and feeling the beating of His mighty heart. I do not disparage the books of the Bible nor the "Evidences"—I respect them. I have sat at the feet of these sacred bards and enjoyed it. But I do not find all the time I desire for this now, I find I have to get a little evidence here and a little there as I can pick it up, and the whole earth is full of proofs of God. The method of science is exact and full, and young men should avail themselves of it if possible. But there are other things to study.

PREACHERS' METHODS.

This world is a world of truth and it is God's truth. Science is a grand conception and truth science is God's Christianity. Christianity needs science, and science needs Christianity. Each must work for the other. Take out the work of educating and transfiguring men and what can science do? It would be wholly gymnastic, giving a man training, but no impulses of life. I am looking on with interest at the battle between science and Christianity and I want the conclusion at which we shall arrive, to be a victory for God. In order to do this our young men must study all these things as well as the Bible. You must know the things well you would meet if you are to overcome it.

Isaac Errett: — There are two or three things of importance to us, and to Bro. McGarvey, that I will call attention to, so that, as the lecturer himself suggested, he may avail himself of them in his lectures at Fort Scott, Kansas. Bro. McGarvey used the term "preaching" without bringing out the thought of "teaching." This is work, men must engage in, in their regular pastoral line. We have had suggestions given us connecting heart-power. No man who preaches two sermons can have any time for generating heart-power. Crowded with pastoral duties all week, one can scarce do himself justice in preparing his sermons. A man, to grow and be strong must get out and preach his sermons five hundred times, and so fertilize his thought and heart. It is unjust to saddle young men on to congregations. The open field is their place. This is where power resides. Walter Scott preached a sermon fifty times before he could satisfy himself. A sermon is not the inspiration or gush of a moment. It comes by degrees, and by processes of time.

Again, as to adopting rules. Bro. McGarvey gave us some excellent hints in this direction. Still we must adopt all rules with this understanding: that some may not fit us exactly. I depended on what Alexander Campbell told me, and came near making a failure of myself. He advised me never to write my sermons; but I found I had to or I could not think accurately. When I attempted to preach them without writing them out first, I found I treated them in a very crude way and I had to go over all the ground again. I have piles of sermons I never preached, but I am satisfied the writing of them helped me to where I am now.

Again, Bro. McGarvey with all his excellent thought concerning various books in the Bible said nothing about the connection between the Old and New Scriptures. Prideaux Connection used to do very well years ago, but such has been the advance made in various departments of Biblical knowledge that it will not serve the purpose now. I know of none I can recommend that meets all demands.

As to the making of sermons I think there are a great improvments still to be made. Young men must avoid the habit of selecting a text and essaying around and about it as Spurgeon does. Men simmer over a text, frequently, no one knowing what they intend when they begin their sermons, nor when they conclude it. I have myself' been pressed into three services daily, and find in such cases I had to adopt some strategy by which I would relieve myself of an excess of study. I brought my congregation together in the afternoon, giving them a short lecture on some section of Scripture and questioning them upon it. Sometimes an essay or two of five minutes length was read, or a word of instruction or exhortation offered by the young men. The people came to this service, Bible in hand, reading or inquiring concerning some difficult passages. From two years' experiment in this direction I found I could make more good preachers than they did at the colleges. I started the men that ought to go to the schools and had them out everywhere with Bible in hand holding prayer-meetings from house to house.

J. A. Dearborn: I have great confidence in Bro. Errett's views as to the course a young man should pursue after being thoroughly prepared by Bro. McGarvey. No greater calamity can befall young men than to take them right out of school and settle them down with old congregations. If you want to diminish a young man to little or nothing this is the plan. If you want to make a man of him take him out of college, put him on a horse and send him over the praries or all through the mountain country. Young men mustn't be always seeking easy places where they can preach two nice little sermons on Sunday. This is not a practical way to develop our young men. Instead of searching round for prominent places let them do good work in the field and these prominent places will be ready for them when they are prepared to take them.

W. S. Priest: I have listened with deep interest to what has been said, but what are you going to do when a struggling church in a city cannot pay large salaries to experienced men. Are you going to let them starve out and die? Supposing a church is not able to pay Bro. Haley or Bro. Jones a thousand or twelve hundred dollars — a sum little enough to be sure for a man who has a family to support — but can raise some young man three or four hundred dollars, what is to be done in this case?

Isaac Errett: Do the best you can. We are considering the matter ideally and I am glad this practical phase has come up. This whole preaching business is a mystery to me. As I get older I conclude I know little if anything about it. One man will go before a congregation with a studied and intelligent sermon, and you would think such intellectuality as he displays would certainly draw immense crowds. Count the people present and very likely he has but a corporal's guard. The other, has nothing but spoon-victuals and he serves this out in a very thin way but you cannot get house-room to hold his hearers. Frequently our own preachers, when at an age from which it is unreasonable to look for much, far excel others of us who have been reading and thinking half a life time.

J. W. M'GARVEY'S REJOINDER.

I have no reply to make. I am glad of all the suggestions and hope to profit by them. I am especially glad to hear Bro. Priest's remarks. Young men get into exigencies as well as old men. They go to college for a year or two, get out of money and have to go to work. Sometimes a good man observes merit in the student and aids him, but this is not often done. The young preacher is bound to go where money is, in such cases, whether it suits his inclination to do so or not. I know no rules in such cases. It is best that he should not bid for mere wealth for this will corrupt him. Let him go out if possible as these brethren advise. Yet, who wants a young student, just from college, to hold them a protracted meeting? If he gets work at all it is often because of the sympathy churches have for him. The tug of war is upon him until he obtains some age and experience, let him do what he will. He must do the best he can and this is all that can be required of him.

INSPIRATION.

BY ISAAC ERRETT.

THE task assigned to me is confessedly difficult. While the *fact* of inspiration is generally admitted, even by those who refuse to acknowledge the Scriptures of the Old and New Testaments as authoritative, the theories concerning the methods and character of inspiration are various and conflicting. It is impossible, within the prescribed limits of this essay, to make a full exploration of these theories; and it would be presumptuous, where so many of the learned have, in their fullest investigations, failed to reach any common ground of agreement, to attempt to dispose of all the difficulties that still throng about the subject in a discussion as brief as the present one must be. The most we can hope to do is to disembarrass the question of some needless difficulties, and point out what seems to us a plainer and safer path of inquiry than is usually pursued.

Our word *inspiration* is derived from the Latin noun *inspiratio*, from the verb *inspiro*, which signifies to blow or breathe in or upon. This corresponds in meaning with the Greek *empneo*. It is easy to see how, in a living language, such a word would glide into various meanings and shades of meanings. Once in the New Testament we have the phrase "inspiration of God," a translation of *theopneustos*, God-breathed, or, inspired of God. "All Scripture is given by inspiration of God" (II. Tim. iii: 16). In our common version of the Old Testament there is just one occurrence of the word *inspiration*. (Job xxxii: 7–8): "I said days should speak, and multitudes of years should teach wisdom; but there is a spirit in man, and the inspiration of the Almighty giveth them understanding." The speaker is a young man, who had been listening to his seniors, and, failing to find in their utterances a solution of the difficult problems involved in the discussion, justifies his own attempt at solution by the remark that while age and experience give wisdom, there is another and higher source of knowledge on such questions, even the divine inspirations — the breathings of God in the soul, which are sometimes vouchsafed to man. He speaks as one who believes himself inspired of God. In the Septuagint we have here *pneuma*, answering to spirit, and *pnoe*, breath or inspiration; as also in Job xxxiii: 4: "The Spirit of God hath made me, and the breath of the Almighty hath given me life." According to Trench,* *pnoe*, conveys the impression of a lighter, gentler breath of air than *pneuma*, and Dr. Curtis suggests that "it is perhaps more occasional and less abiding." As God breathed into the nostrils of man the breath of life, and man became a living soul; so he is spoken of by Elihu as sometimes breathing into the spirit of man knowledge and wisdom, worth more than the lessons of age and experience.

---

* Synonyms New Test. Part II. sec. 28.

We have, in the New Testament, another passage in which the same idea is more fully brought out. It is said of our Lord, that on one occasion, after the resurrection, when in company with his chosen apostles, "he breathed on them, and said unto them, Receive ye the Holy Spirit; whosesoever sins ye remit, they are remitted unto them; and whosesoever sins ye retain, they are retained" (John xx: 21-23).

This must be regarded as a symbolical action, intimating that in order to fit them to make a proclamation of pardon to the human race, the Holy Spirit would be breathed into them. By no wisdom of their own, by no evolution of human nature into a high spiritual perfection, but by a power *from without*, communicated to them, they would be endowed with heavenly wisdom, enabling them to utter God's truth concerning the remission of sins, and to confirm their message by supernatural attestations. Inspiration is not something *breathed out from* man, as the product of his own spiritual culture, but something *breathed into* man — a spiritual illumination from a heavenly source, imparting knowledge and wisdom superior to all that belongs to the subject of it in his natural state, or through his own acquirements.

This inspiration is defined by Knapp as "an extraordinary divine agency upon teachers while giving instruction, whether oral or written, by which they are taught what and how they should write or speak."

Lee declares it to be "that actuating energy of the Holy Spirit, in whatever degree or manner it may have been exercised, guided by which the human agents chosen of God have officially proclaimed His will by word of mouth, or have committed to writing the several portions of the Bible."

Bannerman says: "As an act, inspiration, is the supernatural operation of the Spirit of God upon a man, by which he is enabled to speak or write with infallible accuracy the objective truth revealed to him by God for that purpose. Or, as the result of that act, inspiration is a statement, in speech or writing, made with infallible accuracy, through the supernatural operation of the Spirit, of objective truth revealed to man by God, to be so stated."

Morell, Curtis, and others see nothing in the word but the impartation to man of a superior power to discern and express truth, without involving the idea of infallible accuracy.

These definitions — some of them rather cumbrous — are framed to suit the theories of the writers. Perhaps as clear an idea of its meaning in the New Testament as can be obtained, is found in II. Peter i: 20, 21: "No prophecy of Scripture is of private (or special) interpretation (or exposition). For no prophecy ever came by the will of man; but men spake from God, being moved by the Holy Spirit."

The word rendered *moved*, means *borne along, carried onward*, as a ship by the wind. It indicates a power external to the prophets, by which they were borne along in their utterances. Their prophecies were not their own interpretations of God's will or purposes; but were what the Spirit constrained them to utter — often the meaning of the utterances being unintelligible to themselves.

Now, the fact of such an inspiration is clearly asserted, not only in this passage, but in others which will be hereafter noticed; and may be readily accepted by the believer. But the Spirit's mode of inspiring is quite another thing, and may not be to us explainable. Just here is where the trouble begins. A theory is formed to explain the mode of the Spirit's operations, and the extent to which divine power is asserted over the human mind in these operations. The theory is found to be not exhaustive of the facts in the case. There are facts which it not only does not explain, but actually contradicts. So another theory is formed to overcome this difficulty; but it ignores or contradicts other facts. Coleridge's subjective theory was a revolt from the mechanical theory, but in escaping out of some difficulties, he plunged blindly into others not less formidable. And so we go from theory to theory, and find all of them founded in a partial view of the subject, and oftentimes creating more doubt and perplexity than they remove. It is worth while to raise the question whether a satisfactory theory of inspiration is possible — or whether, as with the subject of the Atonement, a correct philosophy of it is not beyond our grasp. The fact that Christ died for our sins — that he died, "the just for the unjust, that he might bring us to God" — that he "bore our sins in his own body on the tree, that we, being dead to sin, might live unto righteousness" — this fact, we say, is clearly expressed, and the heart can feel its power. But when it is attempted to explain just how it is that the death of Christ takes away our sins—whether his life was a ransom, a price paid down for our redemption; or an offering to divine justice, to make it possible for God to forgive sinners and yet maintain his sovereignty over the intelligent universe; or a display of love to win the hearts of sinful men back to the Father from whom they had strayed; or a seal to the truth he had spoken, by which truth, thus confirmed, men are to be led to repentance—we are at once involved in confusion and strife. The *fact* that Christ died for our sins is submitted to our *faith;* its *philosophy* is beyond the grasp of our *reason.* It might be wise, therefore, to rest contented with the fact, and have as little as possible to do with the theories. As long as a sinner surrenders heart and life to Him who died for him, and trusts him for salvation from sin and death, he is to be accepted to Christian fellowship, whether he accepts or rejects, or remains ignorant of, any or all theories of the Atonement. The *theories* are *human*, the *fact* is *divine*. And as long as any man, conscious of his ignorance of spiritual truth, is willing to accept Jesus as the Way, the Truth, and the Life, and to obey His will, as set forth in the Scriptures, no one has a right to vex him because of this or that theory of inspiration which he holds or rejects. All we have a right to insist on is, that he shall not vex others with his theory, or make it an occasion of strife in the church of God.

It becomes necessary, however, to deal with theories when they are found to be working mischievously. When theories of inspiration tend to destroy confidence in the Scriptures as the revealed will of God, and the foundations of Christian faith are likely to be sapped by the ingenious reasonings of their advocates, it becomes a duty to deal with these theories, expose their errors, and repel their assaults on the Scriptures. It is for this reason, and with no view to add another to the conflicting and confusing theories already existing, that we proceed to note and discuss the leading theories of inspiration now current.

I. *The Theory of Natural Inspiration.* —A theory which admits the fact of inspiration, but traces it to natural causes, denying that there is in it any supernatural element whatever. Thus, Mr. McNaught, of Liverpool, England, following in the wake of Coleridge and Maurice, and pushing their reasonings to the remotest limits, defines inspiration to be " that action of the Divine Spirit by which, apart from any idea of infallibility, all that is good in man, beast, or matter is originated and sustained " (Page 36, second edition). He denies all distinction between *genius* and *inspiration*. He doubts not that " David, Solomon, Isaiah, or Paul would have spoken of everything which may with propriety be called a work of genius, of cleverness, or of holiness," as " works of the Spirit of God, written by divine inspiration" (Page 132).[1]

Mr. Morell, in his " Philosophy of Religion," says: "The proper idea of inspiration, as applied to the Holy Scriptures, does not include either miraculous powers, verbal dictation, or any distinct commission

---

[1] See "Aids to Faith," pp. 346, 347.

from God" (Page 165). On the contrary, it consists "in the impartation of clear intuitions of moral and spiritual truth to the mind by extraordinary means. According to this view, inspiration, as an *internal phenomenon*, is perfectly consistent with the natural laws of the human mind — it is a higher kind of potency, which every man to a certain degree possesses" (Page 166).[1]

Schliermacher, DeWette, and many other German divines, took a somewhat similar view, rejecting all miraculous inspiration, and attributing to the sacred writers what Cicero accorded to the heathen poets — *afflatum spiritus divini* — " a divine action of nature, an interior power resembling the other vital forces of nature."[2]

Dr. T. F. Curtis, while not limiting inspiration to this meaning, finds the basis of it here. He says:

"The mathematical genius of a Newton may be termed inspiration; the elevation of a Milton in his poetry, as well as that of a Bezaleel to design and work in brass for the service of the temple. Did not Pericles and the most eloquent of ancient orators pray for inspiration in their speeches? And have not the supremely wise and good in all ages sought for it in their daily work, and found therein a new and original wisdom leading to the loftiest success? Much of this is, indeed, of a different kind from simply religious inspiration, even where originating in it. But who shall say

---

[1] "Aids to Faith," pp. 345, 346.
[2] See quotation from De Wette in Gaussen, p. 27

that all kinds of inspiration, that of poetry and of the reasoning powers, have not contributed their quota to make our Bibles fit to furnish all men so thoroughly to every good word and work?"[1]

That the word *inspiration* is currently used in the sense of an elevating influence on the intellect or emotions, there is no question. We presume that Pope meant no more than a poetical use of the word in this sense when he said: —

> "O Thou my voice inspire,
> Who touched Isaiah's hallowed lips with fire."

Or Milton, when he wrote: —

> "Sing, Heavenly Muse, that on the secret top
> Of Oreb, or of Sinai, did'st inspire
> That shepherd who first taught the chosen seed."

While he sought the inspiration of the same Spirit that inspired Moses, he meant no more than that he should be granted such an elevation of his intellectual powers as should enable him to grasp and deal worthily with his great theme.

Of this theory we have to say: —

1. Whether anything in the Scriptures is the offspring of such an inspiration as this, or not, it utterly fails to exhaust the meaning of that word in its Scriptural use, or to account for all the facts connected with it. Inspiration is almost uniformly represented as the result of *an influence from without* — the Holy Spirit

---

[1] The Human Element in the Inspiration of the Scriptures, pp 50, 51.

coming upon the persons to be inspired, and *entering into* them, and producing in a moment such a change as enabled them to speak what, before, they could not have spoken; and that, too, in some instances, contrary to their own will, and, in other instances, without a gleam of intelligence on the part of the speaker as to the import of his utterances. We need only refer to instances which we cannot now take space to discuss: That of Balaam (Num. xxiii); that of the prophets who "inquired and searched diligently, searching what or what manner of time the Spirit of Christ which was in them did signify, when it testified beforehand the sufferings of Christ, and the glory that should follow" (I. Peter, i: 10-12); and that of the apostles, who were taught: "Take no thought beforehand what ye shall speak, neither do ye premeditate; but whatsoever shall be given you in that hour, that speak ye, for it is not ye that speak, but the Holy Ghost." These are simple specimens of utterances in connection with the fact of inspiration which cannot be made to harmonize with this theory.

2. The *fact* of inspiration is admitted in this theory. It is not denied that the writers of the Holy Scriptures were inspired. Not only is this not denied, but it is admitted that the inspiration of the Bible, taken as a whole, is greatly superior to that of all other professed holy writings. Thus Emerson says:—

"The most original book in the world is the Bible. This old collection of the ejaculations of love and dread, of the supreme desires and contritions of men, proceeding out of the region of the grand and eternal, seems * * * the alphabet of the nations; and all the posterior writings, either the chronicles of facts under very inferior ideas, or when it rises to sentiment, the combinations, analogies or degradation of this. * * * People imagine that the place which the Bible holds in the world it owes to miracles. It owes it simply to the fact that it came out of a profounder depth of thought than any other book." [1]

Max Müller — and who can speak with more authority on this point? — says, in the preface to the edition of the Sacred Books of the East: —

"Readers who have been led to believe that the Vedas of the ancient Brahmans, the Avesta of the Zoroastrians, the Tripitaka of the Buddhists, the Kings of Confucius, or the Koran of Mohammed, are books full of primeval wisdom and religious enthusiasm, or at least of sound and simple moral teaching, will be disappointed on consulting these volumes. * * * I cannot help calling attention to the real mischief that has been done by the enthusiasm of those pioneers who have opened the first avenues through the bewildering forest of the sacred literature of the East. They have raised expectations that cannot be fulfilled, fears, also, that, as will be easily seen, are unfounded. * * * I confess it has been for many years a problem to me, aye, and to a great extent is so still, how the sacred books of the East should, by the side of so much that is fresh, natural, simple, beautiful, and true, contain

---

[1] The Dial, October, 1840.

so much that is not only unmeaning, artificial, and silly, but even hideous and repellant."

It will be seen, then, that even on this broadest rationalistic theory, the Bible is pre-eminently the Book of books. He who rests his faith upon it, rests on the strongest basis of trust yet vouchsafed to mortals. They who go as far as this in admitting its superior — nay, as far as it is yet known, supreme — inspiration, would they act in harmony with their own concessions and walk in its light, might grow into a nobler faith in this inspired volume.

II. *The Subjective Theory.* — The theory already discussed blends with this, and they might have been discussed together; yet in some respects they are distinct. Dr. Curtis says: —

"The elevation of the Scriptures as a whole, is of course of a higher and nobler kind than the mere inspiration of genius, as it is also higher in degree, though not different in kind, as I apprehend, from that of the Christian, when inwardly moved by the Holy Ghost to consecrate himself as a minister or missionary or translator of the Bible for the heathen."[1]

"By so much as any man is a Christian is he an inspired man."[2]

Let this suffice as a statement of the doctrine of this school of theorists. Inspiration is the result of the elevation of one's spiritual faculties. As Dr. Charles Hodge well remarks: —

"It consists in such an ordering of circumstances

---

[1] Human Element, pp. 51, 52.
[2] Ib., page 48.

and such a combination of influences as to secure the elevation of certain men to a higher level of religious knowledge than that attained by others. They may also, in a sense, be said to be inspired in so far as their inward, subjective state is purer and more devout, as well as more intelligent, than that of ordinary men. There is no specific difference, according to this theory, between inspired and uninspired men. It is only a matter of degrees. One is more and another less purified and enlightened. This theory makes the Bible a mere human production. It confines revelation to the sphere of human knowledge."[1]

Concerning this theory we remark: —

1. Like the theory first discussed, it fails to exhaust the Scriptural meaning of the word *inspiration*, and is at war with many of the facts connected with inspiration in the Scriptures. The cases cited in opposition to the first theory, are equally applicable here.

2. While it is true that God sometimes chose eminently spiritual men through whom to convey lofty spiritual truths, it is also true that some inspired men were of a very different character. Witness Balaam, Solomon, Jonah, and the disobedient prophet (I. Kings, xiii). In none of these instances can it be justly claimed that the inspired men were of lofty spiritual culture or eminent spiritual character. Balaam, "who loved the wages of unrighteousness," and Solomon, with his pride, pomp, sensuality and idolatry, cannot surely

---

[1] Systematic Theology, Vol. I., pp. 172, 173.

be classed with those who possessed elevated spiritual faculties.

Paul certainly admits the possibility of high inspiration without high spiritual elevation, when he says: "Though I speak with the tongues of men and of angels, and have not love, I am become as sounding brass, or a tinkling cymbal. And though I have the gift of prophecy, and understand all mysteries, and all knowledge, and though I have all faith, so that I could remove mountains, and have not love, I am nothing" (I. Cor. vii. 1, 2). He assuredly did not regard inspiration as the necessary result of spiritual exaltation; but on the contrary, considered lofty inspirations as possible in association with inferior spiritual development. To believers in the inspiration of the Scriptures, this passage annihilates this theory. It may be that certain portions of the Scriptures are the offspring of this subjective inspiration; but the theory fails to account for many facts and statements concerning inspired persons, and is not comprehensive enough to cover the whole ground.

3. It is true that the spirit of man is placed *en rapport* with the Spirit of God, only as it is pure. It is true also that "the animal man receiveth not the things of the Spirit — because they are spiritually discerned." But this relates to the *understanding* and *appropriation* of spiritual truth *already revealed*, and not to a knowledge, through divine inspiration, of truths unknown before. There are beauties and glories in nature which are hidden from many, because of their gross tastes and ignorance. Elevation of intellect and edu-

cation of taste may place them on a plane of observation where they may receive and delight in these things, and find a new world open to them. But all these things were already revealed on the pages of the Book of Nature, and were already understood and rejoiced in by multitudes of the intelligent and refined. The purification of our spirits and the resultant fellowship of the Holy Spirit, prepare us to discern spiri ual truths already made known by inspiration, for our own growth in grace and in knowledge; but it does not follow that we are thereby enabled to grasp new truths and communicate new messages of truth and grace and love from God to men. Paul prays in behalf of the Ephesians, that the eyes of their understanding may be enlightened, that they may "know what is the hope of his calling, and what is the riches of the glory of his inheritance in the saints," etc. (Eph. i: 17–23); but these things had been already made known by the inspired apostles, and were simply to be understood and appreciated by the Ephesians, and received into hearts spiritually prepared to receive them. The transmission of truth from God to man is one thing; the study, understanding and appropriation of it is quite another thing. Milton had reference to this moral and spiritual elevation, when he said: —

"And chiefly thou, oh Spirit, that dost prefer
Before all temples, th' upright heart and pure,
Instruct me, for thou knowest * * * * *
* * * * * * * * What in me is dark,
Illumine; what is low, raise and support;
That to the hight of this great argument
I may assert eternal Providence,
And justify the ways of God to man."

While Milton, as the result of intellectual and spiritual culture, might experience such an exaltation of all his faculties and such a quickening of imagination, and of his reasoning powers, as to be able to deal skillfully with the mysteries involved in his theme, he certainly was not gifted to soar into the realm of unknown truth, nor did he bring to earth a single truth unknown before. But men naturally, educationally, perhaps morally, his inferiors, have transmitted from heaven to earth grand truths concerning God and man, sin and righteousness, heaven and hell, time and eternity, duty and destiny; and Milton, with all his intellectual grandeur, was a humble disciple at their feet, learning from them of things which eye had not seen, nor had ear heard, nor had they entered into the heart of man — the things which God had prepared for them that love Him.

III. *The Theory of Evolution.* — This is another anti-supernatural theory. It teaches that in the spiritual as in the material universe, everything proceeds on the principle of evolution. By the operation of this all-pervading law, the highest forms of humanity are evolved from the lowest. Men and peoples begin in savagery and naturally progress into higher life. Every age and nation has its supreme men, its sages, philosophers, poets, and military chieftains — the noblest flowerings of humanity of which the age or nation allows. The highest forms of humanity exist potentially in the lowest; hence there are in the stirrings of its heart, dreams and visions of "the good time coming," prophecies of the glorious destiny of man in the coming ages. They who thus foresee the outcome of humanity's fortunes, and interpret the vague longings of the multitudes, are the seers and prophets of the people, who regard them as inspired of God. The Jews, perhaps more than any other nation, abounded in such gifted men, who were simply more fully developed men than the masses of their countrymen. Their prophets "anticipate the thought of ages by profound intuitions, pregnant imaginations, visions of the seer, as Plato does. Genius often outstrips the plodding feet of generations, but genius must not put on the airs of omniscience."

Rev. R. Heber Newton, from whom the last quotation is made, further says:

"There was, however, a more real and substantial typifying of Christ through the Old Testament, but it was natural, organic, ethical and spiritual, in those books, as first in the lives of the people. The growth of the nation onward toward the true image of God, the true Human Ideal; the travail of the nation with the Divine-Human Character which at the last came to the birth in Jesus the Christ; this was a mystery of natural, organic evolution which 'must give us pause' in every shallow denial of a supernatural involution in human history. This makes true rationalism reverent before 'that Holy Thing' born not alone of Mary, but of Mary's race, begotten plainly of the overshadowings of some Holy Ghost, of whom our best judgment is, now as of old, — 'He shall be called the Son of the Highest.' The whole history of Israel is a growth of The Christ, and that is the abiding wonder of it. In such a mystic evolution it may well be, in history as in nature, that the organic processes type the on-coming form of life."[1]

Thus Jesus the Christ, the Son of God, is himself a natural evolution of humanity — the perfect flower of the ages, "begotten of some Holy Ghost" or other — some one of the various Holy Ghosts which the ages in their progress had produced! Verily, there is little worthy of the name of inspiration in the Old Testament Scriptures, if this is the sum and substance of its teachings. We get rid not only of supernatural prophets, but of a supernatural Christ as well, and, as Dr. Hodge says, " revelation is confined to the sphere of human knowledge." We cannot give much space to the discussion of this theory; but we take leave to say that it does not harmonize with the known facts of history, especially of Bible history, which exhibit nations and peoples, not ascending first from savagery and fetichism to high civilization and monotheism, but descending from monotheism and civilization into gross idolatry and barbarism, or associating high intellectual culture with rank idolatry on one hand, and chilling skepticism on the other. Nor does it harmonize with those significant Bible facts, which exhibit a semi-barbarous people, cut off from intercourse with the most enlightened nations, and ever prone to idolatry, yet possessed of, and perpetuating, from age to age, the most enlightened monotheism, the most exalted revelations of the attributes and char-

---
[1] The Right and Wrong Uses of the Bible, pp. 99, 100.

acter of the one living and true God known in all the religions and literatures of the ages preceding the Christian era.

The theory has, however, a strong semblance of truth, and therein lurks its danger. There *is* a progressive development of moral and spiritual truth thoughout the Old Testament history — a gradual unfolding of the gracious purposes of Jehovah in behalf of our race, until "the fullness of time" when God was manifested in the flesh in the person of Jesus of Nazareth. There was a long reign of night, when the stars twinkled in the heavens; a period of moonlight, when the reflected light of the invisible sun gave to earth gentle and pleasant illumination; to which succeeded the light of the morning star, heralding the approaching day — and then the Sun of Righteousness arose with healing in his wings. The revelations made during that long period were partial — God spoke "by divers portions and in divers manners by the prophets unto the fathers." This must always be kept in mind in the interpretation of the Old Testament. On this point, Mr. Newton has said many just and forcible things under the head of "The Wrong Uses of the Bible." But they do not touch the question of the inspiration of the Scriptures. They have been as well and as earnestly said by others, who profoundly belived in the plenary inspiration of the Old Testament Scriptures. They relate, not to *inspiration*, but to *interpretation*. If the Lord had a revelation to make to children, it would undoubtedly be in the language of children, and would necessarily be a partial revelation, adapted to the capacity of children; but it would require as complete an inspiration to make this partial revelation in language suited to childhood, to make it of its own kind perfect, as would be required for a fuller revelation to men of mature minds, in language adapted to the capacity of manhood. It requires more wisdom to talk successfully to children than to adults. The idea that because the communication is to be made to children, it requires less care or less ability, or fewer safeguards about it to have it serve the highest purposes of truth, is absurd. It must have a form of expression adapted to the infant mind, and it must be within the limits of the child's capacity to understand; but within these limits it must be as true and as trustworthy as communications of a broader or higher nature made to mature minds. The world had its infancy, its childhood, its youth, before the fullness of time arrived; and God's revelations were adapted to the various stages of development in humanity's progress; but they are not, for this reason, less inspired than after revelations.

When we come to consider the views of inspiration entertained through the ages by those who accepted the Holy Scriptures as a divine revelation, we fail to find for a long time, any special *theory* of inspiration. Touching the views held by the ancient Jews, our information is meager. Josephus says: —

"Every one is not permitted of his own accord to be a writer, nor is there any disagreement in what is written; they being only prophets that have written the original and earliest account of things, as they have learned them of God himself by inspiration; and others have written what hath happened in their own times, and that in a very distinct manner also. For we have not an innumerable multitude of books among us, disagreeing from and contradicting one another (as the Greeks have), but only twenty-two books, which contain the record of the past times, which are justly believed to be divine."[1]

There is here nothing more than an assertion of the *fact* of inspiration.

Philo Judæus, while conceding to Moses a superior place among inspired men, evidently regarded all the sacred writers as inspired. Indeed his own system of allegorical interpretation could have had its basis only in such a view of inspiration as gave divine significance to even the slightest word or statement of the Jewish Scriptures.

The story that prevailed among the Jews, to the effect that the translators of what is now known as the Septuagint version did not confer with each other, but carried on their work separately, or in pairs, and that when they met to compare their versions, they were found in every point exactly to agree, goes to show that the ancient Jews profoundly believed in the verbal inspiration of their Scriptures. The tradition may be false, but its acceptance shows what was generally believed concerning even a *translation* of the Scriptures, and their faith in the inspiration of their original Scriptures could not, of course, be less. And it ought

---

[1] Contra Apion, Book I, 7, 8.

to be carefully noted that the Rabbinical authorities quoted to prove that the Jews insisted on different degrees of inspiration among their sacred writers, belong to later times. It is most probable that this theory was adopted in the early centuries of the Christian era to break the force of the Christian argument based on the Jewish prophecies, by assigning to the prophets the lowest degree of inspiration, as knowing only a part of the truth.

Among the Christian writers of the early centuries of the Christian era we find a general and emphatic assertion of the fact of inspiration, but no generally accepted theory of it. As far as their views of the method of inspiration crop out, they prove to be various. Some, like Justin, inclined to a theory of mechanical inspiration, the Divine Spirit "acting on just men as a plectrum on a lyre." Others, like Athenagoras, inclined, to the subjective theory — inspiration being the full flower of personal spirituality. Others, like Tertullian, believed that divine communications were made through men in a condition of trance or ecstacy, the subject being wholly passive. Clement of Alexandria, and others, maintained the existence of an allegorical meaning throughout the whole Bible, which of course, involves verbal inspiration. Origen seems to have inclined to the subjective view, arguing that "the divine messengers, by the contact of the Holy Spirit with their souls, so to speak, gained a keener and a clearer intuition of spiritual truth;" yet, whatever his theory, he evidently believed in the plenary inspiration of the Scriptures. Theodore of Mopsuestia recognized different degrees of inspiration. Augustine seems to have favored what is now called the mechanical theory. These facts are sufficient to show that while the early church profoundly revered the Scriptures, Old Testament and New, as inspired, and as authoritative communications of the will of God, they accepted the fact of inspiration without any settled or prevalent theory as to the *modus operandi* of the inspiring Spirit.

IV. *The Church Theory.* — Before coming to the prevalent orthodox theories, it is proper to note the Roman Catholic theory, which has also lent its influence to some of the Protestant theories.

In the Douay Bible, in a note on II. Timothy iii: 16, we read:—

"Every part of Divine Scripture is certainly profitable for all these ends. But if we would have the whole rule of Christian faith and practice, we must not content ourselves with those Scriptures which Timothy knew from his infancy, that is, the Old Testament alone, nor yet with the New Testament, without taking along with it the traditions of the Apostles, and the interpretation of the Church, to which the Apostles delivered both the book and the true meaning of it."

The Council of Trent decreed (Session 4) concerning the truth and discipline of the Gospel, that they are:—

"Contained in the written books and unwritten traditions which, received by the apostles from the mouth of Christ himself, or from the apostles themselves, the Holy Ghost dictating, have come down even unto us. * * * One God is the author of both (Old and New Testaments), as also the said traditions, dictated either by Christ's own word of mouth, or by the Holy Ghost."

According to this view, inspiration, for all practical purposes, dwells in the Church, rather than in the Bible; that is, whatever inspiration may be allotted to the Scriptures, it is of no avail only as we have an inspired and infallible interpretation of it by the Church; or, according to the ripest development of this doctrine, until we have an inspired and infallible interpretation of it by the Pope.

It does not fall within the range of this essay to discuss this doctrine of inspiration, nor have we the space to do it justice. We dispose of it, therefore, with this remark. It does not rid us of any of the difficulties that throng about the question of inspiration, but rather multiplies them. For, while we have abundance of historical testimony of the decisions of council against council, pope against pope, and even of one edition of the Scriptures with papal approval against another edition of the Scriptures with a similar indorsement,[1] it is evident that we are increasing the difficulties touching alike the questions of inspiration and infallibility by this Church theory.

V. *The Theory of Verbal Inspiration.* — This theory belongs to the seventeenth century. It is, in one of

---

[1] As in the revised text of the Vulgate put forth under the auspices of Pope Sextus V., in 1590, and that of Clement VIII., in 1592.

its phases, called the *Mechanical* theory; and in another the *Mystical* theory of Philo and of some of the Christian Fathers, who regarded the sacred writers as passive and uttering the Spirit's words in a sort of frenzy. The inspired writers were simply machines, used by the Divine Spirit to utter the Spirit's words, without any necessary knowledge of the meaning of their utterances. Some of this school of theorists contend that not only every word, and phrase, and the order of these, but the vowel-points and the punctuation, were dictated by the Holy Spirit. The *Formula Consensus Helvetici* declares that the Old Testament is *theopneustos*, — God-breathed — equally as regards the consonants, the vowels, or at least their force."[1]

Dr. Gaussen in his well-known work on Inspiration, says, in his conclusion: "The whole written word is inspired by God, even to a single jot and tittle." The Holy Spirit, according to this theory, dictated the words and the style, and the sacred writers were merely amanuenses. This is a very simple theory, easily apprehended; but, while it may be admitted that there are instances in which facts seem to support this theory, such as those in Balaam's case, where he was compelled to speak words contrary to his own will, and in the case of some of the prophets, who did not understand what they uttered, and became anxious students of their own prophecies, — the theory is confronted with the undeniable fact that there is in the Scriptures no uniform characteristic of authorship, so far as words

---

[1] Charles Elliott's Treatise on Inspiration, p. 217.

and style are concerned, but on the contrary, the peculiarities of the different writers are marked and unmistakable; so much so that their personal idiosyncrasies and their degree of culture unmistakably appear. In a word, we are compelled to recognize a human element in these productions, to such an extent that while, in view of their inspiration, we properly say, "Thus saith the Lord;" in view of the human element, we may as properly say, thus saith Isaiah, thus saith Micah, thus saith Mark, or John, or Peter, or Paul. As Gaussen himself puts it, in stating the argument of his opponents:

"No one, say they, can read the Scriptures without being struck with the difference of language, conception and style, discernible in their authors; so that even were the titles of the several books to give us no intimation that we were passing from one author to another, still, we should almost instantly discover, from the change of their character, that we had no longer to do with the same writer, but that a new personage had taken the pen. This diversity reveals itself even on comparing one prophet with another prophet, one apostle with another apostle. Who could read the writings of Isaiah and Ezekiel, of Amos and Hosea, of Zephaniah and Habbakuk, of Jeremiah and Daniel, and proceed to study those of Paul and Peter, or of John, without observing, with respect to each of them, how much his view of the truth, his language, has been influenced by his habits, his condition in life, his genius, his education, his recollections — all the circumstances, in short, that have acted upon his outer and inner man? They tell us what they saw, and just as they saw it. Their memory is put into requisition, their imagination is called into exercise, their affections are drawn out — their whole being is at work, and their moral physiognomy is clearly delineated. We are sensible that the composition of each has greatly depended, both as to its essence and form, on its author's circumstances and peculiar turn of mind."

Dr. Gaussen must be credited with fairness and candor, in stating this objection to his theory. And it must be acknowledged that he wrestles with it bravely. But, in our judgment, he is unsuccessful. He says very prettily: —

"As a skilful musician, when he would execute a long score by himself, takes up by turns the funereal flute, the shepherd's pipe, the merry fife, or the trumpet that summons to battle; so did Almighty God, when He would make us hear His eternal Word, choose out from of old the instruments which it seemed fit to Him to inspire with the breath of His Spirit."

This is illustration, and not argument; and it is deceptive illustration, for the analogy must be instituted *between different instruments of the same kind*, and not between *different kinds of instruments*. He might properly take different fifes, or trumpets, or organs, to show that, after all, each instrument, though made by the same hand, and played upon by the same musician, has its own peculiarities; but beyond this he can not properly go. God's inspired ones were all *men;* and if there is no human element in their inspiration they will all give forth the same music at the touch of the hand or the breath of the Divine Performer. This will be seen more forcibly if we recur to the illustration which these theorists are fond of employing. The Holy Spirit is the dictator, and the human writers are mere amanuenses. Now, if amanuenses are simply to take down what is dictated to them by the same person at different times, while there may be a difference in the *penmanship*, and in the *subject-matter*, and differences in adapting style and matter to different persons and peoples, that is as far as the difference will extend. There could be no such differences in the productions of the same author as are found in the productions of the various writers of the sacred books.

But Gaussen really surrenders the position of the mechanical theorists, in admitting, as he does, the unmistakable evidences of *a human element* in the sacred writings. In admitting this, he and those of his school, are compelled to adopt an *accommodation theory* — that the Holy Spirit merely " accommodated Himself" to the peculiarities of the sacred writers. One of them says: " The Holy Ghost inspired His amanuenses with those expressions which they would have employed had they been left to themselves;" thus making inspiration in regard to words wholly useless. Mr. Lee well says on this: —

" This wholly hypothetical statement assumes an exercise of the divine agency for which no motive can be assigned, or end pointed out; while it seems impossible to reconcile this phase of the organic, or as it has of late years been termed, *mechanical*, theory of inspiration with the highest aim of religion — the elevation and enlightenment of the faculties of man.[1]"

We have to remark further concerning this verbal theory, in all of its phases, that it is useless. For even if it were true that every word, as originally spoken or written, was inspired, we have none of the original documents, and the Scriptures are now read in copies containing many various readings, interpolations, omissions, and errors of various kinds; and in translations which, at best, could not always reproduce in another language words and phrases exactly answering to those in the original language, but which, in fact, are often very imperfect. The translations, quite as much as the originals, would need the benefits of verbal inspiration; and although this claim for certain translations has sometimes absurdly been put forth, and multitudes of pious but ignorant people in our own country and in England, until very recently, regarded King James' version with a reverence due only to inspiration, the day is past when such a view can be seriously entertained. Irenæus and Augustine regarded the Septuagint as an inspired translation, and the latter was quite unwilling that its errors should be interfered with; but such a doctrine no longer needs refutation.

It is said in reply, that notwithstanding all the errors in transcribing and translating, and the formidable list of various readings, there is no serious interference with the meaning of the text; that a clear knowledge of the divine will, in relation to the truths to be be-

---

[1] Lee on Inspiration, p. 37.

lieved, the duties to be performed, the evils to be avoided, and the hopes to be cherished, can still be obtained, even from the most imperfect translations; and that practically the Bible is a volume of inspired truth and a safe guide in all that pertains to salvation, duty, and destiny.

All this, we respond, is cheerfully admitted. While the full beauty and strength of some truths may be obscured, and some errors in translation may be misleading — as a whole, the Bible, in any translation, is a safe guide to a knowledge of spiritual truth and duty. More than this: the progress of textual criticism, the careful and critical collation of manuscripts, and their scientific classification, is rapidly relieving us of doubt and uncertainty and bringing us on to more solid ground as to the original text. As a rule we feel no uncertainty as to the *thought* — " the *mind* of the Spirit," as communicated in the holy writings. This we are glad to be able to say. But, so far as the precise words are concerned, the facts we have mentioned, and which no one disputes, explode the theory of verbal inspiration, and prove it to be practically useless. If it had been the divine plan to give heavenly communications in God's own words, rather than God's thoughts in man's words, there would have been needed the same inspiration for copyists and translators as for the original speakers and writers; for it must have been known to the Divine Mind that these communications would go out to men mostly in copies and translations of the originals. The fact that no such inspiration was ever granted, and is no longer even pretended, is itself proof that God did not purpose, in inspiration, anything beyond a transmission of His *thoughts* in the *words of men*. His providence has so far watched over the Scriptures of truth that "the mind of the Spirit" has been preserved, even in imperfect translations, sufficiently to furnish a safe guide to man; while the errors that have been committed by human hands, and the uncertainties attendant upon human carelessness, short-sightedness, and even partisan zeal and bigotry, have compelled such critical and anxious explorations in the fields of Biblical literature as to stimulate those who revere God's word, and even those who reject it, to the employment of their noblest powers in the study of the Bible, resulting in an intellectual strength, an enlightened faith, and a spiritual vigor, that could have been realized in no other way.

We do not assert that in no instances has God employed men merely as amanuenses; but we do affirm that this theory does not and cannot account for some of the most prominent and universally recognized facts involved in the question of inspiration.

VI. We ought here to say that *plenary* inspiration does not necessarily involve verbal or mechanical inspiration; although they are often confounded. Plenary inspiration affirms that *all* Scripture is inspired. Dean Alford was pronounced in his opposition to the verbal-inspiration theory, but holds to plenary inspiration. It may not be amiss to give a specimen of his reasoning.

"*The Title on the Cross* was written in Greek, and being reported in Greek by the evangelists, must represent not the Latin or Hebrew forms, but the Greek form of the inscription. According, then, to the verbal-inspiration theory, each evangelist has recorded the exact words of the inscription; not the general sense, but the inscription itself — not a letter less or more. This is absolutely necessary to the theory. Its advocates must not be allowed, with convenient inconsistency, to take refuge in a common-sense view of the matter whenever their theory fails them, and still to uphold it in the main. And how it will here apply, the following comparison will show:

Matthew: This is Jesus the King of the Jews.

Mark: The King of the Jews.

Luke: This is the King of the Jews.

John: Jesus of Nazareth the King of the Jews.

"Of course it must be understood that *I* regard the above variations in the form of the inscription as in fact no discrepancies at all. They entirely prevent our saying with perfect precision what was the form of the inscription; but they leave us the spirit and substance of it. In all such cases I hold with the great Augustine when treating of the varying reports of the words spoken by the apostles to our Lord during the storm on the Lake of Galilee: 'The sense of the disciples waking the Lord and seeking to be saved, is one and the same, nor is it worth while to inquire which of these was really said to Christ. For whether they said any one of these three, or other words, which none of the evangelists has mentioned, but of similar import as to the truth of the sense, what matters it?'"

That is, so as we get the idea, why higgle over the words? But Dean Alford proceeds to say:—

"If I understand *plenary inspiration* rightly, I hold it to the utmost, as entirely consistent with the opinions expressed in this section. The inspiration of the sacred writers I believe to have consisted in the *fullness of the influence* of the Holy Spirit specially raising them to, and enabling them for, their work, in a manner which distinguishes them from all other writers in the world, and their work from all other works. The men were full of the Holy Ghost — the books are the pouring out of that fullness through the men — the conservation of the treasure in earthen vessels. The treasure is ours in all its richness; but it is ours as only it can be ours, in the imperfections of human speech, in the limitations of human thought, in the variety incident first to individual character, and then to manifold transcription and the lapse of ages."

Alford approaches most nearly —

VII. *The Dynamical Theory* — Which insists on "the infallible certainty, the indisputable authority, the perfect and entire truthfulness of all and every part of Holy Scripture;" but fully recognizes the human element — the Holy Spirit enabling the inspired person to speak and write without interfering with his liberty and self-control. It is not attempted to explain how this union of human and divine agencies is effected. As in the living, incarnate Word, the human and divine were united, the divine and human sustain a similar relation to each other as in the person of Christ. "They are unmixed," says Dr. Schaff, " yet inseparably united, and constitute but one life, which kindles life in the heart of the believer." We may not be able to separate the divine and the human; they may be so blended as to defy analysis; but " the two agencies — the divine and the human — employed in the composition of the Scriptures, are so combined as to produce one undivided and indivisible result." As Dr. Charles Eliott says: " Notwithstanding the exercise of human agency in writing the Bible, it is all alike divine; and notwithstanding the divine agency employed in its composition, it is all alike human. The divine and the human elements together constitute a theanthropic book." This theory involves *plenary* inspiration — that is, the inspiration of *all* the Scriptures, making the Bible as a whole a *complete* revelation of the will of God, and of the truth he designed to communicate to men. In one respect this theory needs to be carefully guarded. In saying that all Scripture is inspired, the conclusion instantly drawn by the ordinary mind is, that *everything in the Scriptures is true*. Yet we know that in the Book of Job, for instance, a great many erroneous things are said, and even Job himself had to acknowledge his errors. That the book, as a whole, teaches important truths, and that the writer may have been inspired to set forth all these errors for the sake of correcting them and bringing out the truth in full force, may be admitted; but when it is argued that these errors are inspired utterances, and that which is shown in the end to be false is taken to be God's own truth, the results are necessarily mischievous. It is said of a New York judge, that in his charge to the jury at a murder trial, he stated that " we have *the highest authority* for saying, 'All that a man hath will he give for his life;' " thus quoting Satan as " the highest authority!" It may be sadly true that oftentimes, in our courts, Satan *is* the highest authority; but the judge in this case was evidently misled by the prevalent error that whatever is in the Bible came from God, and must be true. In Ecclesiastes, we have the sentiments and arguments of a sensualist and a materialist introduced — with a view, indeed, to show their baseness, and to lead the mind of the reader out of this slough of atheistic sensuality and up to the conclusion that the whole happiness of man is "to fear God and keep his commandments ;" but if the utterances of a sensualist are to be taken as inspired, it is easy to see what evil results must follow. Indeed, it is not uncommon to quote as God's own truth, from the books I have mentioned, and as scriptural proofs that man dies like a beast, the declarations of men who certainly were not inspired, but spoke their own false conceptions; though it may yet be true that the writer was inspired to place these things on record. In both Old and New Testaments we have genealogical records which whoever asserts their inspiration will find a puzzling task on his hands. Inspiration may have led to the copying of such records as sufficient for the purpose had in view, and in this sense plenary inspiration may, perhaps, be affirmed; but there is a call for careful discrimination at this point.

In view of these and other difficulties, some writers have adopted a theory, which does not, as far as we can see, necessarily war with the dynamical theory, namely : —

VIII. *The Theory of Degrees of Inspiration.* — We do not now refer to the theory wrought out by Maimonides concerning the Jewish Scriptures, but to Christian writers, such as Bishop Wilson and Dr. Henderson. Dr. Wilson, Bishop of Calcutta, enumerates the inspiration of " suggestion, direction, elevation, and superintendency;" and Dr. Henderson makes a different classification, viz. : " Divine excitement, invigoration, superintendence, guidance, and direct revelation." Without approving either classification, I may be allowed to say that if we are going to theorize at all on this question, my conviction is that, in order to cover all the facts involved, and give an exhaustive definition of inspiration, we shall be compelled to recognize some such distinctions. There is no need to contend for more inspiration than is needed in any given case; and we take it, the needs vary according to circumstances. It surely did not require the same supernatural endowments to select and copy chronicles and genealogies from State archives, as to unfold the eternal purpose of God in the moral government of the universe, or to make known the hight and depth and length and breadth of that love of God which, indeed, " surpasseth knowledge." If the Song of Solomon is to be accepted as an inspired book, we see not how to class its inspiration with that which produced the Epistle to the Romans; nor can we honor the parable of Jotham (Judges ix: 7–20), or the imprecatory psalms, with a place alongside the Sermon on the

Mount. Paul spoke "according to the wisdom given unto him" (II. Peter iii: 15), and David and Solomon according to the wisdom given unto them; and the wisdoms are different. To Jesus the Spirit was given "without measure;" to others it was given by measure, and the measures varied. Unless this fact is recognized, we do not see how any satisfactory explanation of inspiration can be made — if, indeed, it can be satisfactorily explained at all.

We have thus sketched the various theories of inspiration that seem to us worthy of note — not in all their phases, but in generalizations sufficiently comprehensive to group together all that possess essentially the same characteristics; and have attempted to point out, not all their defects, but their failure to meet the just demand that a theory must satisfactorily dispose of, or account for, all the known facts belonging to its subject. This prepares the way for the second lecture, in which we propose to inquire into the true ground of our belief in the inspiration of the Scriptures, and to set forth what we regard as the true path of inquiry to conduct us to safe conclusions.

LECTURE II.

Inspiration, whatever may be its rank in point of *importance*, is not by any means first in order in our inquiries after religious truth. It is not a question that ought to meet us at the threshold of our inquiries into the truth of Christianity. He who accepts a challenge to discuss this as a preliminary question, is led into a false position, and allows the enemy to take an undue advantage of him. The first question relates to Jesus himself — his person, his character, his official relations; his person as the Son of God; his character as consistent with his dignity as a Divine personage; his official relations as "the Christ," the Anointed Prophet, Priest and King, coming from God to instruct, redeem, and reign in and over the human race. "What shall we do with Jesus, who is called the Christ?" is the question first to be disposed of. And we respectfully submit that it may and should be disposed of without raising the question of inspiration. All that is necessary as preliminary to a rational settlement of this question is, an agreement to admit the books that contain a record of the life and character of Jesus as authentic and genuine, submitting them to the same grammatical and critical tests that are insisted on in the case of any other historical documents. As trustworthy witnesses, and not as inspired messengers, the four Evangelists must be appealed to in this first inquiry. Nothing more than this is needed; nothing more should be demanded. If the inquirer after the truth concerning Jesus, is already a believer in the truth of the Old Testament Scriptures, this is a decided advantage; but it is not essential to a settlement of the question concerning the Divinity or the Christhood of Jesus that he should even know there is such a book as the Old Testament. Many of the original converts had but little knowledge of the Old Testament; some of them were absolutely ignorant of it. Paul at Athens did not quote Old Testament prophets, but heathen poets; nor did he raise the question of his own inspiration. The human testimony concerning Jesus, tested by all the laws applied to other human testimony, must settle the question as to his life, character, teaching, death, resurrection, and exaltation to the heavens. If this does not lead to faith in him as a Divine Lord and Saviour, it is vain to raise the question of inspiration — a waste of time to discuss it. These testimonies were written for this purpose. "These are written that ye might believe that Jesus is the Christ, the Son of God, and that believing ye might have life through His name" (John xx:31).

An examination of these testimonies led Nicodemus to say: "We know that thou art a teacher sent from God, for no one can do these miracles that thou doest except God be with him."

A study of the unique and transcendent character of Jesus constrained Ernest Renan to confess: "Whatever may be the surprises of the future, Jesus will never be surpassed. His worship will grow young without ceasing; his legend will call forth tears without end; his sufferings will melt the noblest hearts; all ages will proclaim that, among the sons of men, there is none born greater than Jesus."

A careful study of his life and his work led Frances Power Cobbe to say: —

"One thing we must believe — that he to whom was committed such a work, he to whom such a part was assigned in the drama of history by its great Author, must have been *spiritually* of *transcendent excellence*. Of ordinary genius, or powers of any kind, he may have had less or more; but of those hidden faculties *by which the highest religious truths are reached*, and of that fervent loyalty by which the soul is fitted to receive divine instruction — of these Christ must have had a superabundant share. Strictly to define his spiritual rank, he must surely have been *the man who best fulfilled all the conditions under which God grants his inspiration.*"

A study of the diction of the writers of the four Gospels, and of the teaching they record, led Rousseau to write:

"The Jewish authors were incapable of the diction, and strangers to the morality contained in the gospel. The marks of its truth are so striking and inimitable, that the inventor would be a more astonishing character than the hero."

And in the same strain Theodore Parker declares:—

"It would have taken a Jesus to forge a Jesus."

"He pours out a doctrine beautiful as the light, sublime as heaven, and true as God. The philosophers, the poets, the prophets, the Rabbis — he rises above them all. Yet Nazareth was no Athens, where philosophy breathed in the circumambient air; it had neither Porch nor Lyceum; nor even a school of the Prophets. There is God in the heart of this youth."

"Eighteen centuries have passed since the tide of humanity rose so high in Jesus: what man, what sect, what church, has mastered his thought, comprehended his method, and so fully applied it to life?"

Even David Frederick Strauss, with all his mythical extravagances, is compelled to confess:—

"To the historical person of Christ belongs all in his life that exhibits his religious perfection, his discourses, his moral action, and his passion. * * * *He remains the highest model of religion within the reach of our thought;* and no perfect piety is possible without his presence in the heart."

Such are the tributes paid even by unbelievers to the supreme excellence of Jesus as a teacher of morals and religion, on the basis of the testimony of the four Gospels, regarded as uninspired documents. To the mind simply prompted by a desire to know the truth, and unembarrassed by the prejudices of theorists already committed to a denial of the supernatural, it may readily be seen how these testimonies are sufficient to inspire them with a faith like that of Peter, when he cried, "To whom shall we go? thou hast the words of eternal life; and we believe and are sure that thou art the Christ, the Son of the living God."

Having settled, without inspiration, this greatest of questions, we have now the true starting point in our search for unquestionable proofs of inspiration. On the voluntary admissions of such rationalists as we have quoted — and we could greatly multiply such quotations — it is apparent that Jesus, as the most highly inspired of our race, is the best judge of the inspiration of others. Where he recognizes inspiration, it would be presumptuous in those who recognize in him the highest and deepest inspiration in spiritual things, to set up their feeble judgment against his.

And on the part of those who are led, on the testimony submitted to them, to accept Jesus in his true character as the Christ, the Son of God, there can be no hesitation in accepting as inspired all that he accepts or promises as such. Thus, in this, as in all other moral and religious problems, the solution is found in Jesus. He is the answer to every inquiry, the solver of all doubts, the final demonstration of every truth — "the Way, the Truth, the Life."

What, then, do we learn from Jesus, on this question of inspiration?

1. Touching the inspiration of his own messengers, sent to the world with his message of salvation, we have from him very clear statements. In a passage already quoted in the former lecture (Mark xiii:11), he told his apostles that when, in preaching the gospel, they should be delivered up to councils, or be brought before rulers and kings, they should not premeditate a speech, "but whatsoever shall be given to you in that hour, that speak ye, for it is not ye that speak, but the Holy Ghost;" or, as Luke expresses it, "The Holy Ghost shall teach you in the same hour what ye ought to say" (chap. xii:11); and again (chap. xxi:14, 15), "Settle it therefore in your hearts, not to meditate before what ye shall answer; for I will give you a mouth and wisdom which all your adversaries shall not be able to gainsay or resist." Notice that this was not something to be developed *out of* them, as the result of their spiritual education, but something to be *put into* them, and that in the very hour when they were to break. As foreshadowing or symbolizing this impar-

tation of a heavenly gift, to enable them to announce authoritatively the conditions on which God would forgive sins, Jesus breathed on his apostles, and said unto them, "Receive ye the Holy Ghost; whosesoever sins ye forgive, they are forgiven unto them: whosesoever sins ye retain, they are retained" (John xx:22, 23). All this is more fully explained in our Lord's last conversation with these apostles, before his agony in the garden of Gethsemane.

"But the Comforter, even the Holy Spirit, whom the Father will send in my name, he shall teach you all things, and bring to your remembrance all that I said unto you" (John xiv: 26). "It is expedient for you that I go away; for if I go not away, the Comforter will not come unto you; but if I go I will send him unto you. And he, when he is come, will convict the world in respect of sin, and of righteousness, and of judgment. * * * When he, the Spirit of Truth, is come, *he shall guide you into all truth*, for he shall not speak from himself, but what things soever he shall hear, these shall he speak, and he shall declare unto you the things that are to come" (John xvi: 7, 8, 13, 14).

Here note:—

(1.) That this Spirit of truth was not to be developed *from within*, but sent upon them *from without*.

(2.) By the inspirations of this Spirit, (*a*) all that Jesus had said and done was to be brought to their remembrance; (*b*) they were to be guided into all truth; (*c*) the things of the future were to be revealed to them.

Take in connection with this the facts narrated in Acts ii., and succeeding chapters in that book, — not the culmination of their spiritual culture, but a sudden endowment of spiritual wisdom and power from on high — and it is impossible to escape the conclusion that these apostles, in proclaiming the gospel, in announcing the terms of pardon, and in teaching the way of truth and life to their converts, were divinely inspired — guided by a God-breathed power and wisdom, which gave to their utterances and their proceedings, in fulfilling their divine commission, divine certainty and divine authority; so that we may safely apply to them under their final commission, the words of our Lord addressed to them when they were first sent forth on a local mission : " He that receiveth you, receiveth me; and he that receiveth me, receiveth him that sent me" (Matt. x:40). For, as their divine teacher said in his intercessory prayer, " The words which thou gavest me I have given unto them; and they received them; and knew of a truth that I came forth from thee, and they believed that thou didst send me" (John xvii:8). Paul was not included directly in these promises and declarations; but I need not stop to prove to those who accept New Testament statements, that he is virtually included in them, and that what was true concerning the other apostles, so far as inspiration is concerned, was true also of him. We have, then, the highest authority for pronouncing the teaching and preaching of the apostles, whether oral or written, divinely inspired. It is not our business now to inquire into the genuineness and authenticity of the apostolic writings. That is a question totally different from this which we are now discussing. Our argument goes to show that whatever these apostles wrote or spoke in fulfilling their commission was under the guidance of the Spirit of truth; that divine inspiration necessarily inheres in their teaching. Therefore, unless they specially disown it in reference to any of their utterances, or the circumstances attendant on those utterances are such as to show unmistakably that they spoke merely from themselves, we are bound to accept what they say, in fulfilling their apostolic charge, as the word of God. This settles, also, the inspiration of two of the four evangelists; for Matthew and John were apostles, under the guidance of the Holy Spirit. Michaelis and others reject the inspiration of Mark and Luke, since they were not apostles. Of this we may have a word to say hereafter.

II. What do we learn from Jesus touching the inspiration of the Old Testament Scriptures?

Without attempting to be exhaustive — our space forbidding this — we submit what we think will be sufficient on this point.

1. "All things must needs be fulfilled, which are written in the law of Moses, and the prophets, and the psalms, concerning me. O foolish men, and slow of heart to believe in all that the prophets have spoken! * * * And beginning from Moses, *and from all the prophets*, he interpreted to them *in all the Scriptures* the things concerning himself" (Luke xxiv: 44, 45, 25, 27). Whether the classification of the Jewish Scriptures by the more modern Jews into the Law, the Prophets and

the Holy Writings, prevailed in our Lord's time, we are not able positively to say. But Jesus recognized "the law, the prophets, and the psalms," and these are equivalent to "all the Scriptures," according to Luke. We know, from Josephus that the Jewish Scriptures contained twenty-two books; and it is pretty well settled that our thirty-nine books embrace no more than the twenty-two books of the Jews. Now Jesus recognized "all the Scriptures," and expounded them. He recognized their inspiration, inasmuch as they were instinct with the *spirit of prophecy*, for they spoke of the things concerning him. This accords perfectly with what he said on another occasion: "Ye search the Scriptures, because ye think that in them ye have eternal life." This must be taken as including all that the Jews acknowledged as Scripture. He adds: "And these are they which bear witness of me" (John v : 39).

2. In another instance, our Lord places "Moses and the prophets" on a high plane as books of inspiration. "They have Moses and the prophets; let them hear them. If they hear not Moses and the prophets, neither will they be persuaded if one rose from the dead." (Luke xvi : 29–31). To make Moses and the prophets equivalent in moral power, as asserting the presence and authority of Jehovah, to the miracle of resurrection, is certainly to assert of them what can only be true as involving their divine inspiration.

3. He recognizes these Scriptures as "the word of God," in opposition to the traditions of the elders —

the doctrines and commandments of men. See Matt. xv: 1–13; Mark vii: 1–13.

4. He quotes from Moses, as speaking by inspiration (Matt. xxii: 31, 32); from David (Ib. 43–45; John x: 34, 35); from Isaiah (Matt. xv: 7–9). These cannot be regarded merely as instances of applying the *argumentum ad hominem*.

5. He refers to the historical Scriptures as authority: with reference to the creation of the original pair (Mark x: 6); Noah and the deluge (Matt. xxiv: 37–39); Abraham (John viii: 39, 40); Isaac and Jacob (Matt. viii: 11); Lot, Sodom and Gomorrah (Luke xvii: 28–32); David (Matt. xii: 3); Solomon, the queen of Sheba, Jonah and the Ninevites (Matt. xii: 40–42); Elisha and the widow of Sarepta, and Naaman (Luke iv: 25–27): the lifting up of the serpent (John iii: 14); the manna (John vi: 58); and so on. This wide range of reference from Genesis onward shows that Jesus accepted the Old Testament history as authoritative — as fact and not fable, as indisputably true, and not as a mixture of truth and falsehood. Let us add that his *regular custom* of attending at the public worship in the synagogue, reading the lessons, and expounding the Scriptures read (Luke iv: 16–32), is not capable of satisfactory explanation on any other supposition than that He regarded these Scriptures as the word of God. He never intimates a doubt concerning any of these Scriptures, but he most pointedly and emphatically denounced all additions to these as "doctrines and commandments of men," as plants which his heavenly Father had not planted, and which

must be rooted up (Matt. xv: 9–13); while of the "Scripture," he declared that it "cannot be broken" (John x: 35), and that not even a jot or tittle should pass from the law till all was fulfilled (Matt. v:18).

The fact of the inspiration of the Old Testament Scriptures is, then, established by the most competent witness in the universe — Jesus Christ himself; unless it can be shown that some of the books now embraced in those Scriptures did not anciently belong to them. We must not omit to say — what really has great force in it — that the testimony of Jesus is not testimony as to any particular book or books. He regards these sacred writings *as a whole* as possessing *a unity of purpose* — as written to *testify of Him*; so that the history, the types, the prophecies, all link together in a chain of divine revelations that reach from Genesis to Malachi, unfolding the eternal purpose of God.

Concerning those books of the New Testament not written by the Apostles — Mark, Luke and Acts — for we do not entertain here the question of another authorship than that of Paul for Hebrews, or than that of Peter for what is known as his second epistle — there is this to be said: that what we know of the close relation of Luke to the apostle Paul, and what tradition has preserved of a similar relation of Mark to Peter, ought to banish all serious doubt as to the character of the books they wrote. Others besides apostles were inspired. The apostles themselves bestowed spiritual gifts on others, and it is not reasonable to suppose that the needful spiritual gift would be withheld from these intimate associates and trusted men. As far as internal evidence goes—and that is a chapter we cannot enter on here — it is as weighty in behalf of these as of the other biographers and historians; and the unanimous decision of the early Christians, who evidently sifted with care and decided with caution upon the claims of various lives of Christ, in favor of Mark and Luke along with Matthew and John, leaves no good reason to doubt that they are entitled to the place they occupy as writers under the guidance of the Spirit of Truth.

If, now, I am asked to reconcile this view of the inspiration of the Scriptures with alleged contradictions in the sacred writings, with contradictions between Bible statements and alleged facts of science, and with the doctrine of the "higher criticism" concerning the authorship of the books called the books of Moses, I answer: This is no part of my present duty. I am seeking the true grounds of the claim of inspiration for the Old and New Testaments. If I am correct in the view I present, then the Bible must stand or fall on its merits as an inspired volume. If the alleged contradictions cannot be disposed of; if the teachings of science, in opposition to the teachings of the Bible, cannot be met and answered; if the most modern school of Old Testament criticism cannot be silenced; then it may be that the claim of inspiration for these Scriptures will have to be abandoned, and more than that — the infallibility of Christ's teachings may have to be surrendered also. I will say, however, that on this score I have no fears. We have passed through such trials before. There is nothing more threatening now than on some former occasions, in the attitude of natural scientists and Biblical critics. The conflict has not yet resulted in overturning the claims of the Bible as a book of divine inspiration. When what is extravagant in the claims of science and criticism, on one hand, shall have been surrendered, and what is unauthorized in the text of the Scriptures and in the interpretation of Scripture, shall have been abandoned on the other hand, it will be found that we have lost not truth, nor inspiration, nor science, nor sound, enlightened criticism, but simply the errors that were incorporated with these. Scientific theories come and go, but Nature endures; the schemes of critics and the systems of theologians may rise, and flourish, and fade, and perish; but "the word of the Lord endureth forever."

This leads us to a final inquiry: Admitting the fact of inspiration, have we in the inspired Scriptures an *infallible* guide? Are they absolutely free from error? That all truth is infallible needs no proof. But, is the *communication* of truth, in the inspired Scriptures, absolutely free from error? I do not see how we can answer this question affirmatively, unless we can prove that human language furnishes an absolutely certain method of communication between mind and mind. Nor do I see how this can be proved.

That human language, spoken or written, may, for all practical purposes, be accepted as a trustworthy medium of communication between man and man, may be freely admitted. It is, indeed, almost the sole medium of such communication. Were it withdrawn, there would not only be an immediate arrest of human progress, but a rapid descent of the race into a savagery worse by far than any that has ever been known in its history. Language is one of the mightiest agents of civilization. All the quickening power of thought and passion is conducted by it from mind to mind, and from heart to heart. Love and hate are expressed in it; laws are embodied in it; history, philosophy, poetry, are embalmed in it; nations and races are held together by its mystic power; it leaps from the glowing heart of the military chieftain on the battle-field, and instantaneously kindles an answering flame of enthusiasm in the hearts of his soldiers, and inspires them for death or victory; it goes forth from the anointed lips of the orator, and sweeps with resistless power over the souls of his hearers, swaying them as the trees of the forest are swayed by the sweep of the tempest; it breaks out in song on the lips of the minstrel, and goes echoing down the centuries, and the inspiring strains, caught up by generation after generation, intensify national pride, patriotism, and the love of liberty; it utters the wisdom of sages, the reasonings of philosophers, the imaginations of poets, the appeals of the patriot, the lessons of the statesman, the inspirations of the prophet; and even the unutterable mysteries of love seek to reveal themselves through its gracious ministries. A single sentence telegraphed from some great center of commerce, may thrill millions of hearts with hope or despair, and change the currents of commercial life all around the world. We trust language as a vehicle of thought in all the most important and sacred affairs of life. Personal fortune and reputation, family peace and happiness, social enjoyment and security, the interests of agriculture, manufactures and commerce, of literature, art and science, of philanthropy and statesmanship, and the national and international interests of humanity, find in language their chief servitor — their indispensable reliance. Without it man would deteriorate into a grinning, scowling brute, and all the fair forms of civilization would perish.

We need not wonder, then, that God, in seeking to communicate with man, chose human language as the vehicle of his thoughts; that this universally trusted channel of human communication and fellowship should also become the channel of divine communication to our race, and the medium of fellowship between the heart of God and the heart of man. We find, accordingly, that out of all the magazines of His power — out of all of His infinite resources — the All-Wise selected human language as the most trustworthy means of conveying the enlightening, converting, and sanctifying power of the heavens to the conscience and heart of man.

The great Pentecostal gift, was therefore, the gift of tongues; tongues of fire were the symbol of the regenerating and sanctifying power of the most perfect spiritual dispensation yet established to promote the highest spiritual interests of humanity. That which we can trust in all the most sacred and precious of human interests, through which we draw to our present aid all the inspirations of the past and the future, and on which we rely not only for our individual growth and advancement, but for the growth and advancement of our race, we may also safely trust in regard to our spiritual interests, and rely on for our growth into an immortal spiritual manhood, and for the accomplishment of the high purposes of God concerning the destiny of our race. We have, I must think, a right to conclude that the universe does not afford any other as safe and satisfactory means of communication between God and man, or as perfect a medium of conveyance of God's moral power to the human heart, as is found in human language.

But while this is true, we must not be blind to the fact that human language has limitations as a medium of communication between mind and mind. With all its advantages, and notwithstanding its absolute necessity, it is still an imperfect method of conveying thought between man and man, even in regard to the ordinary affairs of life. Much of the discord of life and many of its bitter controversies and wide-spread alienations, are traceable to this source. As Bishop Butler says: "The imperfections attending the only method by which nature enables and directs us to communicate our thoughts to each other, are innumerable. Language is, in its very nature, inadequate, ambiguous, liable to infinite abuse, even from negligence, and so liable to it from design, that every man can deceive and betray by it."[1] If this is true of language, even as a means of communication between man and man in regard to earthly things, it must be

---

[1] Analogy, Part II., Chap. iii.

especially true of it as a means of expressing the truth concerning the invisible, the infinite and the eternal. From the very structure of the constitution of the human mind, and from the nature of language as adapted to our mental structure, abstract truths, things invisible and unknown, can only be expressed analogically or metaphorically; and here at once the way is open for misinterpretation.

1. Let it be considered that the ancient Hebrew had not over six thousand words, and these, according to Max. Müller, have been reduced to about five hundred roots.[1] It will be seen that, of necessity, one word must often be pressed into service to express a great variety of meanings, and these frequently departing so far from the original meaning as to seem to have no connection with it. Prof. Roberts, in his recent work on Old Testament Revision, states that "the one word *Tor*, which in its fundamental signification, seems to imply 'arrangement,' also signifies 'a way of acting,' 'a turn,' 'a string of pearls,' 'a turtle dove,' and 'an ox.'"[2] And M. Renan points out that the one word *Room*, which expresses the idea of *hight*, has given rise to the following related, yet widely divergent meanings; to rise, to strengthen, to lift up, to build a house, to educate, to place in safety, to render conqueror, to extol, to speak loud, to levy tax, to raise hurriedly, to offer sacrifice, to cherish pride, a hill, a heap, haughtiness, a sacrifice, a gift.[3]

---

[1] Lectures on Language (1st ser.), p. 297.
[2] Page 9.
[3] Ibid.

It will be seen that such a language must be of a highly metaphorical character, and that the liabilities to mistake must be greatly increased when such a language undertakes to express abstract truth, or to convey intelligence concerning the unseen and unknown.

2. Consider that "the great characteristic of Semitic speech is the tri-literal composition of its words. Almost all the verbal forms consist of three letters — neither less nor more. And these letters are all *consonants*, the vowels being left unwritten, as of comparatively little consequence."[1] There is here such an opening for mistake as to preclude the idea of absolute certainty and infallible accuracy. The vowel points had an unknown origin. Even as eminent a Hebrew scholar as Dr. Lightfoot claims for them divine inspiration. But such a view is no longer seriously entertained. There is, therefore, no refuge from uncertainty in the painstaking system of vowel-points, elaborated, if not originated by the Massorets. "The most diverse significations attach themselves to words, according to the vowels by which their consonants are attended." Take along with this the use of Hebrew *accents* as a means of punctuation, and the influence of punctuation in deciding the meaning of sentences; and we cannot say that we are helped in our search after absolute certainty in the Hebrew text of the Scriptures.

3. Consider that the most ancient Hebrew manuscripts yet known cannot be dated much higher than the tenth century of the Christian era;[2] that "the

---

[1] Roberts, Old Testament Revision, page 2.
[2] Roberts O. T. Revision, page 152.

science of Old Testament textual criticism is still in a comparatively imperfect condition;" and that in the judgment of most modern Hebrew scholars, "all copies of the Hebrew text go back to one archetypal text," which had become fixed among the Jews some time after the birth of Christ,[1] and that "the real character of the existing Hebrew text as respects absolute trustworthiness is, as yet, undecided,"[2] and we must surely hesitate to say even of the Hebrew text as it now stands, that it is the infallible word of God.

4. Add to this, what was said in the first lecture concerning Greek as well as Hebrew manuscripts, and concerning New Testament as well as Old Testament manuscripts, mistakes of copyists, and imperfections and errors of translators. We are compelled in view of all these considerations, to insist on limitations when the language of Scripture is spoken of as characterized by infallible accuracy. From the imperfect character of human language itself, especially from its inadequacy to express fully the truth concerning spiritual things; from the poverty and imperfections of the Hebrew language in particular; from the absence of certainty in regard to the Hebrew text; from the fact, that language as a science is not yet a hundred years old; from the acknowledged errors of transcribers and translators; from the numerous variations in existing manuscripts; we are compelled to decide against the infallible verbal accuracy of the Scriptures, and against all claims of

---

[1] Roberts, page 138.
[2] *Ib.* page 140.

infallibility that leave out of view the limitations of imperfection that inheres in language itself, and of inaccuracy that necessarily belongs to human transcription and translation.

If, in response to this, it be said that, notwithstanding the acknowledged imperfections of human language, and the accidents always possible to that which is placed in human keeping, such language is, nevertheless, a trustworthy means of communication between man and man, and we reasonably rely on it in the most important affairs of human life and destiny— in matters of friendship, of love, of education, of commerce, of civil government, of literature, science, and art, and find it a safe reliance even in the most difficult and critical questions of life and death; we rejoin: All this is freely admitted, and we may safely trust it as equally trustworthy as a means of communication between God and man. Nay, admitting the writers of these Scriptures to have been inspired, we may say that, for substance, the Bible is much more trustworthy than any merely human expression of truth. That, as a rule, critics have been successful in detecting interpolations and sifting out the truth from the various readings; that errors of translation have been, in the most important cases, exposed and rectified; that, amidst all the risks in the preservation of manuscripts, no important truth has ever been allowed to perish, no duty has ceased to be made plain; that we have, substantially, "the word of God," "the mind of the Spirit," even in the worst translations; and that the Bible is, therefore, even in imperfect translations, a safe guide to the knowledge of God's will and our duty: all this we rejoice to be able to express as our settled conviction. But this does not remove the limitations of which we have spoken. It simply shows that, in spite of these limitations, human language is a trustworthy means of communication between men, a wonderful and mighty instrument of enlightening, purifying, and ennobling humanity, and of leading it on to a grand earthly destiny; and that it may be at least equally trustworthy as a means of expressing the thoughts of God, of regenerating and sanctifying human nature, and of guiding it to a destiny of glory, honor and immortality.

That God has chosen the best means of conveying his will to man, and that as far as human language is capable of expressing truth with completeness and certainty, and in adaptation to the capacities of those to whom they were addressed, the Scriptures are an infallible revelation of divine truth, and are, for all practicable purposes, an accurate and trustworthy guide; this is our conclusion. But we repeat that this must be held subject to all the limitations of which we have spoken, growing out of the nature of language, and the fortunes of the Scriptures in careless or ignorant or prejudiced hands for so many generations.

That God has spoken to man; that his messengers spoke as they were moved by the Holy Spirit; that the same God who spoke at various times and in various manners unto the fathers, has in the last of the appointed ages of time, spoken to us by his Son; that what was written aforetime was "written for our learning, that through patience, and through comfort of the Scriptures, we might have hope "(Rom. xv : 4); and that all the inspired Scriptures are " profitable for teaching, for reproof, for correction, for instruction which is in righteousness, that the man of God may be complete, furnished completely unto every good work : " these are Scripture affirmations which may be accepted in all their fullness, without insisting either on verbal inspiration, or on any such absolute infallibility as would ignore the limitations which we have already mentioned and discussed.

We ought, perhaps, to explain that we have done no more than allude, hitherto, to the passage in II. Tim. iii: 16, 17, which by many is regarded as the ground on which the battle for the inspiration of the Scriptures must be fought and settled as a philological question, or as a question of interpretation. We have kept this text in the background for two reasons: 1. We think the question of the inspiration of the Scriptures can be more satisfactorily settled by the broad treatment it has received in these lectures than by any argument based on a single text, the correct translation of which is, at this time, a matter of dispute. 2. The question of translation, with reference to this text, cannot be satisfactorily discussed within our limits. We take occasion now, however, to say that we do not attach much importance to the dispute over the translation of this passage. Whether we read, " Every Scripture inspired of God is also profitable for teaching," etc.; or, "All Scripture is given by inspiration of God, and is profitable," etc., in either case the reference is to the "holy Scriptures" spoken of in verse 15, which Timothy had known from his childhood, and which were able to make him wise unto salvation through faith in Christ Jesus. That these were the Jewish Scriptures, and the Jewish Scriptures as a whole, is, we believe, admitted on all hands. It is of these Scriptures as a whole that Paul asserts that all inspired writings are profitable for the uses mentioned; and this is only another form of asserting — what we have already quoted from Romans — that "whatsoever things were written aforetime were written for our learning." We see no need, therefore, for a strife of words here. It is of more importance to note what is clearly affirmed in this passage — that the sphere of inspiration is the sphere of moral and spiritual truth, and not that of physical science or of intellectual philosophy.

Nor have we paid the least attention to the distinction adopted by several recent writers from the Franciscan monk, Claude Frassen, of the seventeenth century — though really of much earlier date — between *revelation* and *inspiration*, because (1) while it may be a convenient classification in behalf of certain theories, and may sometimes be just, the distinction is, after all, more fanciful than real, since what is styled revelation is often the highest order of inspiration, and it is at best a question of *degrees of inspiration*, and not of revelation as something entirely distinct from inspiration; (2) we notice that those who adopt the distinction differ as to what belongs to revelation and what to inspiration; the distinction, therefore, is arbitrary, and tends to confusion. It has been our object to relieve the question of inspiration, as far as possible, of all needless encumbrances, and of this, therefore, along with many others.[1]

Of the things we have spoken, this is the sum: —

1. By general consent, and on any hypothesis, even the most broadly rationalistic, the Bible, as a whole,

---

[1] In the discussion which followed the delivery of this lecture, it was pointed out, with some justice, that we had failed entirely to notice the important passage in I. Cor. ii: 13, which, it is claimed, fully asserts the doctrine of verbal inspiration. Our failure was not an oversight, but grew out of the fact that we had not space to discuss properly this text, and others of importance, and our essay was not designed as an exhaustive discussion of any of the theories mentioned. Nor can we do more now than make a suggestion or two on this passage. It reads as follows: "Which things also we speak, not in the words which man's wisdom teacheth, but which the Holy Ghost teacheth." We observe that, whether the contrast here is between the gospel and Grecian philosophies, or between the gospel and the arts of rhetoricians and orators, in either case the idea is not that any of these were taught or expressed in the very words in which they had been received, but that human wisdom *had a language of its own*, and so had divine wisdom. This is true; but verbal inspiration does not necessarily follow. To press the term *logoi* in this narrow sense does not seem to us to be warranted. When our Lord said (John xvii: 8): "I have given unto them the *words* which thou gavest me," did he mean that he repeated, word for word, the words given unto him by the Father, and that the apostles would repeat, word for word, what he had taught them? When the Gentiles at Antioch in Pisidia requested that "*these words* might be preached to them the next Sabbath," did they mean that the *very same words* should be used, or that the same *things* — the same *thoughts, ideas, arguments*, should be repeated to them in words befitting the theme? The latter, undoubtedly. That the wisdom of God *has a language of its own*, befitting its nature, is what Paul asserts; but it does not follow that verbal inspiration is necessary.

must be regarded as a book of inspiration — of divine inspiration; and in this respect superior to any other book or collection of books known in the entire range of religions and religious literature.

2. Jesus Christ, as unapproachable in the fullness and richness of his inspirations — in his superhuman insight into moral and spiritual truth, is necessarily the highest authority as to inspired persons and inspired books.

3. On his authority, the Old Testament Scriptures, as they were found in his day, were inspired; also, the speeches and writings of his apostles.

4. The various *theories* of inspiration belong to modern times, while the *fact* of inspiration has been recognized in all ages. All these theories are unsatisfactory, inasmuch as each one fails to cover all the facts concerning inspiration which the Scriptures supply. There may be some truth in every theory we have had under discussion; but the whole truth is found in none of them.

5. Any assertion of infallibility as belonging to the inspired Scriptures must be subject to the limitations growing out of the imperfections of human language and the uncertainties and perils ever attendant upon materials placed in human custody, and subject, more or less, to the control of ignorance, credulity, prejudice or superstition.

6. As a trustworthy communication of the will of God, in all that pertains to salvation, righteousness and holiness, or to human duty and destiny, and as a safe and sure guide in all the ways of truth and right-

eousness, the Bible is entitled to our untrembling confidence and acceptance; and, in this regard stands alone among all books in the world.

It would please us, if we had the space, to vindicate the statement last made by an examination of the internal evidences of inspiration which the Bible furnishes, and of the influence of this book upon human nature and upon society, wherever that influence has been fairly asserted. Unable to attempt this, we must be content to submit, from one who scouts this view of inspiration, — and whose admissions are on this account all the more weighty — a single paragraph on these points: —

"Of all books of which we have any knowledge, those together constituting the Bible form incomparably the most potent factors in the moral and religious progress of the western world; and as all other progress is fed from moral and religious forces, I may add, in the general advance of Christian civilization. From these books the lisping lips of children have learned the tales of beautiful goodness which have nourished all noble aspirations. Over these charming stories of Hebrew heroism and holiness, the imagination has caught sight of the infinite mysteries amid which we walk on earth. Their touch has quickened conscience into life. Through their voices the whispers of the Eternal Power have thrilled the soul of youth, and men have learned to worship, trust, and love the Father-God. These books have preserved for us the story of the Life which earth could least afford to lose, the image of the Man who, were his memory dropped out from our lives — our religion, morals, philanthropy, laws and institutions, would lose their highest force. These books have taught statesmen the principles of government, and students of social science the cardinal laws of civilization. The fairest essays for a true social order which Europe and America have known, have laid their foundations on these books. They have fed art with its highest visions, and have touched the lips of poesy that they have opened into song. They have voiced the worship of Christendom for centuries, and have cleared above progressive civilization the commanding ideals of Liberty, Justice, Brotherhood. Men and women during fifty generations have heard through these books the words proceeding from out the mouth of God, on which they have lived. Amid the darkness of earth, the light which has enabled our fathers to walk upright, strong for duty, panoplied against temptation, patient in suffering, resigned in affliction, meeting even death with no treacherous tremors, ha ; shone from these pages. In their words young men and maidens have plighted troth to each other, fathers and mothers have named their little ones, and by those children have been laid away in the earth in hope of eternal life. All that is sweetest, purest, finest, noblest in personal, domestic, social and civic life, has been fed perennially from these books. The Bible is woven into our very being. To tear it from our lives would be to unravel the fair tapestry of civilization — to run out its golden threads, and crumble its beautiful pictures into chaos." [1]

---

[1] Rev. J. Heber Newton's Right and Wrong Uses of the Bible, pp. 7-9.

All this being true, we are safe in receiving the Bible, "not as the word of man, but, as it is in truth, the word of God, which effectually worketh in them that believe."

It is our safe and sure guide through tne uncertainties and perils of mortal life to the land of immortal glory and eternal blessedness. To lose faith in it is to abandon the soul to uncertainty, bewilderment and despair. Heaven may have something better in store for us. Our emancipated and glorified spirits, dwelling in the light of God, may employ their unfettered capacities in the study of truth under conditions that will make such revelations as these unnecessary; but, under the limitations of our present existence, the Bible is our indispensable guide, and we do well to heed it as "a light shining in a dark place, until the day dawn, and the day-star arise in our hearts."

REMARKS ON THE PRECEDING LECTURES.

By J. W. McGarvey: Much the greater part of Bro Errett's elaborate essay meets my unqualified approval;

NOTE BY THE EDITOR:—It was suggested at the lectureship that Bro. McGarvey should be requested to write out his address himself, and then let Bro. Errett reply to it in writing. This had been acted upon by the committee. On examining the two papers it seems best to forego the privilege of publishing the other speeches made in this discussion for two reasons: (1) while they were prompted in the main, by things said either by Bros. Errett or McGarvey, these two brethren, in what will appear, are chiefly concerned with each other's points; and (2) because it is putting the other speakers at a disadvantage to report what they said on the spur of the moment, side by side with *elaborated* thought. It has cost us some concern and disappointment to do this, and the more because some *good* things were said by *good* men. But, on the whole, we think they will commend our action. Only such allusions remain in the two addresses as are needed to convey to the public the complete line of thought. Both these men are masters in what they treat, and we can now give our undivided attention to the issues joined.

but at two points he came into direct antagonism with my settled convictions, and in reference to these I wish to speak as briefly as I can.

It seems to me that the only value attached to the question of inspiration is its bearing on the question of infallibility. The majority of the theories which the lecturer stated and so effectually refuted, were conceived by men who denied the intallibility of the Scriptures and framed their theories in harmony with this denial. I was pained to hear from Bro. Errett the concession that the Scriptures are not infallible. In arguing the necessity of this concession, he really argued a totally different question. His mind seemed unconsciously to drift from the question whether the original record is infallible, to the question whether the thoughts contained in it are conveyed infallibly to our minds. He discussed the fallibility of translations, of copied manuscripts, and of interpretations; and he insisted upon the variety of meanings belonging to certain words; but he said nothing at all, that I remember, on the infallibility of the original autographs. No scholar claims infallibility for any translation, or for any Greek or Hebrew manuscript. No one outside of the Roman Catholic priesthood claims the power of infallible interpretation. When we affirm the infallibility of the Bible, we mean only this: that its thoughts were so expressed as to be conveyed infallibly to minds which correctly understand the words employed. We mean, that such words were selected and such sentences and paragraphs were formed, as to furnish an infallible expression of the thoughts intended. On this question we heard nothing in the lecture, and consequently all that was said on the subject of infallibility appears to me to have missed the mark at which it was aimed.

The objections which the lecturer urged against verbal inspiration are, to my mind, equally invalid with those urged against the doctrine of infallibility. That God has not seen fit to grant verbal inspiration to copyists, translators, and interpreters is no proof that he did not grant it to the original writers. Neither does the fact that interpreters, translators and copyists are left without such aid, render the verbal inspiration of the original writers useless, as Bro. Errett has argued. It has left us without a divine help which we might have gladly accepted; but if verbal inspiration is a reality we have an infallible original to which we can be perpetually making nearer and nearer approaches, and which enables us, so far as we certainly find its meaning, to be that far infallibly correct. This is an immense gain, one of incalculable value, compared with having an original which is itself clouded by human fallibility. If the sacred writers were left to their own choice of words, and their own construction of sentences, we know that some uncertainty attaches to their writings, and, what is worse, we know not how to locate this uncertainty in any given place, but are compelled to let it spread like a mist over the whole Bible. This conception robs us of certainty in regard to everything. It takes away certainty even from the apostolic commission, for, if this theory be true, who can affirm with entire confidence that Jesus ever said, "He that believeth and is baptized shall be saved."[1]

What the lecturer said about Hebrew words possessing a great variety of meanings undoubtedly presents an obstacle in the way of the translator and the interpreter; but I cannot see that it presents any in the way of verbal inspiration, or of infallibility in the original writer. Even if a word has forty meanings, he who uses it may know infallibly in which one of the forty meanings he employs it, and the Spirit of God within him may lead him to employ it in such connection with other words as to convey this meaning unmistakably to the reader. If I had to believe that in such instances the Bible writers were left entirely to their own construction of sentences, I would feel a degree of uncertainty as to the result; but if I can be sure that they were divinely guided in both the choice and the location of words, I can rely implicitly upon the exact truthfulness of all they have written.

The only way to ascertain the truth, and the whole truth, on this subject of inspiration is to first examine carefully what the Savior promised in the way of inspiration, then examine, with equal care, what the apostles claimed for themselves and others in fulfilment of this promise, and finally to take into considera-

---

[1] In the discussion which followed this speech it was urged that some uncertainty does attach to this passage on account of doubts as to its genuineness; but, while this proves that my selection of it was not a happy one, it does not meet the issue made, seeing that a passage of undoubted genuineness would have answered my purpose as well.

tion all the facts presented in the Scriptures which in any way may limit or modify the promises and statements previously examined. I cannot take time to even attempt such a treatment of the subject in these remarks; but, with the indulgence of the Association, I will call attention to a few things in this line of thought which I think should greatly modify the lecture to which we have listened with so much interest.

Bro. Errett has already called attention to the words of our Savior in which he charged his apostles that when brought before governors and kings they should not premeditate nor be anxious as to how or what they should say; that, in other words, they should not premeditate either the matter or the manner of their speeches. The reason given is, that "it is not ye that speak, but the Spirit of your Father that speaketh in you." I understand this latter expression as an example of the well known Hebraism by which the absolute is put for the relative, and that the meaning is, it is not you alone that speak, but the Spirit of your Father, and the Spirit chiefly that speaketh in you. They spoke; and it is impossible, in reading their speeches, to avoid the conviction that mind and heart were both actively engaged in all that they uttered. But, if the Savior's promise was realized, it is absolutely certain that in all they said the Spirit bore a part, guiding and directing them how to speak and what to speak.

It was a most singular thing to prohibit men, when about to answer for their lives, from premeditating what they should say. Were I required to answer as Paul did before Agrippa and Festus, I would be extremely solicitous as to what I should say, and I would select with the utmost care every word I was about to speak. The wording of my thoughts would give me no less solicitude than the thoughts themselves. But Paul was forbidden to bestow any forethought on either, because of the promise that it should be given him what he should say, because it was the Holy Spirit who should speak in him. This promise includes verbal inspiration in all its fulness.

But notwithstanding this, when we examine the speeches delivered in fulfilment of this promise, we find in them all those chraacteristics which have been regarded by some theorists as evidence that there was no miraculous inspiration at all. Before Agrippa, Paul begins by expressing his gratification at being permitted to speak before one who was acquainted with the customs and questions among the Jews; he proceeds to speak of having been educated in Jerusalem, and declares that after the straightest sect of their religion he had lived a Pharisee. The whole speech is but a recital of past events which lay on the very surface of his life, and there is not a thought in it which was not as familiar to him as the alphabet. What need had he of the Holy Spirit's aid in order to make such a speech as this? I can see absolutely none, unless it be to guide him in selecting out of the multitude of well re-. membered facts in his past life the few which he mentions, and in choosing the inimitable wording in which these facts are presented. The whole, however, is so perfectly natural to the man, that no one would think that he had divine aid at all, were it not for the promise of Jesus, which could not fail. If it be said that he had no need of the Spirit's aid to choose the words he uttered, I answer that he had still less need of its aid to choose the thoughts; and if there is any evidence here against verbal inspiration there is the same evidence against any inspiration at all. Indeed, you will find this to be true everywhere. Even in the case of the imprecatory psalms, which are considered by many incompatible with the idea of verbal inspiration, the real difficulty is with the sentiments uttered, with the thoughts expressed, and not with the words employed. Clothe the sentiments in any other words, and the apparent incompatibility still remains. The same is true of the different forms of the inscription on the cross, and of all other apparent discrepancies in the gospels and other books. We have seen that John, in his form of the inscription, or Pilate in one of his, inserts the words "of Nazareth" after Jesus. And why? Unquestionably, it is to describe Jesus more fully by giving the place of his former residence. It was an additional thought which required the additional words; and when this variation is arrayed, as you have heard it in the lecture, against the idea of verbal inspiration, it strikes with still greater force against any inspiration at all; for the words would not have been there but for the thought which they express.

We have heard verbal inspiration spoken of under the opprobrius title of *mechanical* inspiration, as though it contemplated the inspired man as a mere machine. But you cannot make a mere machine out of a living man. He is made of heart and mind as well as flesh and blood, and when he is inspired, his whole being, with all his varied faculties and powers, is awakened into activity. He thinks, he feels, his memory is active, his imagination is aglow, his logical powers are grappling with the strong points of his arguments; he is the breadth of the heaven away from a mere machine, and yet, if the Savior's promise is true, he speaks not a word without the guidance of the Holy Spirit. This is a profound mystery, which no one who has not experienced it can understand. It is like the union of the divine and human in the person of Jesus. He never did anything as a mere man, nor anything as exclusively a divine being. In all that he said and all that he did the human and the divine were perfectly blended. So I presume it was with inspired men when speaking or writing as the Spirit moved them. They were themselves in every respect, in their modes of thinking and reasoning, in their emotional nature, in their style and diction, in their tastes and habits; and yet in all that they said, without being led out of themselves they were miraculously guided by the Spirit of God.

It was freely admitted by the lecturer, and it is a fact which cannot be denied by any brother before me, that in some instances on record there was in the strictest sense a verbal inspiration. When the apostles on the day of Pentecost spoke in languages which they had never learned, what kind of inspiration was this? Did the Spirit give them the thoughts, and allow them to choose the words? This speaking in tongues occurred not only at Jerusalem, but in all the churches planted by the apostles; and as we may gather from the first epistle to the Corinthians, in some if not in all of these instances, the man who spoke in a tongue was not able to translate what he had said into his own tongue. This shows that the words were given him without the thoughts; for if he had received the thoughts he could have repeated them in his own language. Again, when the prophets gave utterance to predictions the meaning of which they afterwards sought to understand, what kind of inspiration was this? And when the Apostle Peter himself gave utterance to a promise on the day of Pentecost, the full meaning of which he never apprehended until years after, when he was called by miraculous visions to the house of Cornelius, what kind of inspiration was this? Unquestionably, in all these instances the words were given by the Spirit, while the thoughts were but imperfectly apprehended, or not apprehended at all.

Finally, on this point, I call attention to a declaration made by Paul which Brother Errett has totally overlooked — and I am surprised that he has done so, for nothing escapes him when he studies a subject as he has this. It is a declaration in which, if Paul had intended to affirm the fact of verbal inspiration so explicitly that it would be impossible to misunderstand him, he could not have expressed himself more clearly than he has. Speaking of the things which God prepared for them that love him, things which eye saw not, and ear heard not, and which entered not into the heart of man, he says: "God revealed them unto us through the Spirit."

This shows how the apostles obtained knowledge of these things. But that which was thus revealed to them they spoke to others. Paul adds: "Which things also we speak, not in words which man's wisdom teacheth, but which the Spirit teacheth." Now here is a clear distinction made between the things revealed, the facts and thoughts which make up the matter of revelation, and the words in which those facts and thoughts were communicated by the inspired men. These words, it is expressly declared, were taught by the Spirit and not by the wisdom of man. In view of such a declaration, I dare not doubt the absolute verbal inspiration of the apostles.

And now, with the unquestionable fact before us that the apostles, the prophets, and other inspired men did receive verbal inspiration, who shall say that they ever spoke or wrote in their official capacity without it? They never say so themselves. They do affirm for themselves verbal inspiration, in the most explicit terms; they never make the most distant allusion to speaking the thoughts of the Spirit in words of their own choosing; and as they are as silent as the dead on this latter method of speaking, what facts can justify us in affirming that they ever spoke or wrote in this way? I confess that in all my reading and reflection on the subject I have never found such facts. Sometimes, it is true, the Spirit appears to us to have had the least possible part in what they said, as when Paul asked Timothy to bring his cloak, his parchment and his books; while at others, as in case of speaking in tongues, the Spirit appears to do all, scarcely any part of the man except his vocal organs being employed; yet if we believe the promises of Jesus and the declarations of the apostles, neither the divine Spirit nor the human was ever totally inactive in the choice of any word, the framing of any sentence, or the introduction of any thought found in the writings or speeches of inspired men.

This view of the subject justifies the prodigious labors of such men as Griesbach, Tischendorf, Tregelles, Westcott, and Hart, in eradicating from the sacred text every change made by human hands, and restoring to the world every syllable of the inspired original; it justifies the patient toil of the great host of translators and interpreters who have helped us to understand the original documents; and it enables us to rest with implicit faith upon all the precious words of our blessed Bible; but no other hypothesis enables me to find solid ground on which to place my feet.

ISAAC ERRETT'S REJOINDER.

I had hoped that my lectures would be subjected to a much more searching and thorough criticism than they have received. The question of inspiration is beset with much difficulty, and, until more satisfactory conclusions shall be reached, anything like dogmatism is out of place. I was anxious not only to avoid dogmatic airs, but to receive light from my critics, for my own profit, as well as for the profit of others. It will, however, require longer time, and a better understanding of some of the views set forth in the lectures, for the ripe criticism which is needed.

One of my critics did not hear the first lecture. Had he heard it, he would have been saved the trouble of making the point that Christ himself was not inspired, and that this fact upsets *my* theory; for he would have known that I submitted no theory, but merely showed that none of the prevalent theories cover all the facts in the Scriptures touching inspiration. I showed, in opposition to what is called the *natural* theory, that in a great majority of instances the Scriptures represent the inspiring power as *coming upon* and *entering into* the subjects of it *from without;* and that this theory did not account for, or harmonize with these facts. Now, if it can be shown that in certain instances, speakers or writers made their utterances without any such visitation of the Holy Spirit, and simply as the result of the exaltation of their own spiritual nature, or, as is affirmed by one of my critics concerning Christ, as the result of the perfect knowledge possessed by the *Logos*, I have to say that this is no reply to anything said by me, for I offered no theory. For aught in my lectures to the contrary, there may be instances of *natural* inspiration in the Scriptures. Especially in the poetical and devotional portions of the Bible, there may be much that is the outflowing of cultivated and sanctified imaginations and hearts, wrought out of the actual experiences of the writers, and on that account especially valuable to us as meeting us on the plane of our own struggles, defeats and victories. It may be, too, without warring with any position taken by me, that Jesus did not speak by inspiration. This, if true, would simply exclude His utterances from the sphere of our investigations. But I take leave to say that when it is asked, Did the *Logos* need to be inspired? we are invited on to ground where we must step very carefully. Was the *Logos* ever hungry, or weak, or in the need of sympathy? Yet we know that He of whom it is affirmed that He was the Word made flesh, did, in the flesh, hunger and thirst, and grow weary, and seek the sympathy of his friends. And it is equally clear that, as a teacher sent from God, and as a man standing among men to make known the will of God, he was inspired by the Holy Spirit.

In one of the clearest pedictions of the Messiah, it is said: —

"And the spirit of Jehovah shall rest upon him;
The spirit of wisdom and understanding;
The spirit of counsel and strength;
The spirit of the knowledge and the fear of Jehovah.
And he shall be of quick discernment in the fear of Jehovah;
So that not according to the sight of his eyes shall he judge;
Nor according to the hearing of his ears shall he reprove.
But with righteousness shall he judge the poor,
And with equity shall he work conviction in the meek of the earth
   (Isa. ix: 2-4)."

And our Lord himself quotes from the same prophet (chap. lxi:1), and declares it to be fulfilled in Him. (Luke iv:18-21):

"The spirit of Jehovah is upon me,
Because Jehovah hath anointed me.
To publish glad tidings to the meek hath he sent me;
To bind up the broken-hearted;
To proclaim to the captives freedom;
And to the bounden perfect liberty."

In connection with this let me say, touching the distinction sought to be made between *revelation* and *inspiration*. I do not doubt that such a distinction, properly made, would be helpful; but as it now stands, I think there is more confusion created by it than it removes. For, as stated in the second lecture, revelation, as it is distinguished, is often the highest degree of inspiration; and those who adopt this distinction are not agreed as to what belongs to revelation and what to inspiration. For this reason I ruled it out, as serving to embarrass more than to relieve the mind of the inquirer, and as being incapable of satisfactory treatment within our limits.

In what follows I deal with the criticisms of Bro. McGarvey, much the most direct and complete of any that were offered, and for the directness and force of which he will please accept my thanks. It is not surprising that the impressions made by one hearing of the lectures were, in some respects, dim and imperfect. He certainly has failed to catch the exact meaning of much that I said.

He represents me as conceding that the Scriptures are not infallible. What I said was, that they are not *absolutely* infallible; that when we assert their infallibility, it must be subject to the limitations growing out of the imperfections of human language, its incompetency to convey thought with absolute correctness and perfection, especially concerning things invisible and infinite; also, subject to the limitations of uncertainty growing out of transcription, translation, etc. That we have, in the language of Scripture. a trustworthy source of knowledge of divine things, and a certain infallible guide to salvation, duty and destiny, as complete as language can make it, I distinctly affirmed; but insisted that any assertion of infallibility must be subject to the limitations mentioned.

It is complained that in arguing the necessity of this concession I really argued "a totally different question" drifting from the question whether the original record is infallible, to the question whether the thoughts contained in it are conveyed infallibly to our minds in copies and translations; that I said nothing on the infallibility of the original autographs.

This simply shows that one hearing of an argument is not sufficient, even to one as closely attentive and as capable of grasping an argument as is Bro. McGarvey. The lectures, as delivered, will show that I devoted several pages to a discussion of the nature and powers of human language, and of the Hebrew language in particular, to show the imperfection of language as a means of communicating thought from mind to mind, so that *absolute* infallibility could not be claimed for such communications. It is a great mistake, therefore, to say that I failed to touch the question at issue. I regret that I was so misunderstood at this point, that my argument, somewhat fully stated, has escaped attention, and consequently has met with no reply.

It is true that I did afterwards submit a second argument, addressed to those who assert that we have *now* the infallible word of God, to prove from the errors of copyists, and translators, and from corruptions of the original text, intentional and unintentional, that the asserted infallibility of the Scriptures, as we now have them, is without a firm basis. This, I understand my critic, to concede fully. In admitting this, he puts an end to controversy on the point of highest practical importance to us — for we have not one of the original autographs, and if infallibility cannot be asserted of the Scriptures *as we have them*, or as we may *now obtain them*, there is surely little value to us in a discussion concerning documents which are not, and probably never will be, in our possession.

To make this matter unmistakably clear, I ask Bro. McGarvey, Is this volume — King James' Version — the infallible word of God? He answers, No. Is the Revised Version, or the American Revised Version, or any other English version, the infallible word of God? No. Is the Vulgate in any of its editions? No. Is the Septuagint? No. Is any existing Greek text entitled to this distinction? No. Have we a Hebrew text that can lay claim to infallibility? Still it is anwered, No; we affirm infallibility only of the autographs of the inspired writers. My reply to this is twofold: 1. We have none of the autographs, and a discussion of their infallibility is practically of little value. 2. If we had them, I should still insist, from the inability of human language to convey thought from mind to mind with absolute certainty, that any assertion of their infallibility must be subject to the limitations of the imperfections of human language as a medium of communication between mind and mind. Language, tasked to its utmost, lacks the capacity to convey, with absolute perfection, the conceptions of the Infinite mind; there are passages in which the words are so burdened with the weight they bear that you can almost hear them groan aloud in the tremendous effort to accomplish their task. Nevertheless, that human language was the best medium of communication, all things considered, at God's command, and that, for all practical purposes, the Scriptures are a trustworthy and infallible revelation of moral and spiritual truth, is what has been clearly and repeatedly affirmed in my lectures.

Now, concerning verbal inspiration — which means, as used by my reviewer, that every word uttered by inspired persons, and the arrangement of their words into sentences, was by divine dictation — this is asserted only of the original speakers and writers; it is not claimed for copyists and translators. It cannot then, have been of much importance, for God knew that an immense majority of those to be brought under the power of this revealed truth would receive it in copies and in translations. The fact that verbal inspiration does not belong to these, is evidence that it is not, in divine estimation, essential to an understanding of revealed truth or to an appropriation of its saving power; otherwise, copyists and translators could have been inspired. That it is important to arrive as nearly as possible, at the exact words used by the sacred writers, whether there was verbal inspiration or not, is not in question; for, in any case, the exact words they used must be to us the most certain revelation of truth possible to be reached. But I fail to perceive the force of the plea for verbal inspiration that was made at this point to Bro. McGarvey's criticisms. He says, we are robbed of certainty as to the very terms of salvation, if verbal inspiration is denied. To this I reply: 1. Verbal inspiration is *not* denied where it can be shown to be necessary. I have simply sought to show that the theory of verbal inspiration does not cover all the facts concerning inspiration; I have not denied, but on the contrary have affirmed, that in many cases we have verbal inspiration. 2. In giving the terms of salvation, the inspired writers have not expressed them in their own words, but have given *the words of Jesus*, which were brought to their remembrance according to the promise made to them. (John xiv:26.) 3. Even this does not rescue these declarations from uncertainty, for none knows better than Prof. McGarvey that the passage he quotes (Mark, xvi:15, 16), has much uncertainty attached to it, being under ban, in the judgment of many of the most learned and competent critics, as an interpolation! While I incline, with increasing confidence to the opinion that its integrity as a portion of the text will be finally vindicated, it is impossible to avoid the admission that there is a much greater uncertainty belonging to it than could possibly arise from the mere rejection of the theory of verbal inspiration. 4. If verbal inspiration is so essential in this case, how does it come that the announcement of the terms of salvation has such marked verbal differences as we find, for instance, in Matthew and Mark? Nay, they are found in the announcement of the same terms, at different times, by the same inspired persons. Compare Acts ii:38, with Acts iii:19. The very same conditions and promises in both cases, uttered by the same person in the same city, to the same class of hearers, only a few days apart and yet verbally so different. Is there any uncertainty occasioned by the expression of the same truths in different words?

The instruction to the apostles not to premeditate their speeches, and the promise that it should be given them at the moment what they should say, does not, in my judgment involve verbal inspiration. It is not uncommon, at this day, for speakers, under the pressure of some peculiar excitement or inspiration, to utter their thoughts and feelings with a felicity of diction and a power of expression far surpassing anything they would be capable of preparing by premeditation. We could give numerous instances of this. Yet they choose their own words, free from all dictation. And it may be well supposed that the apostles, all aflame with the inspiration of the divine Spirit, with every intellectual and spiritual faculty vivified, would express the thoughts imparted to them by inspiration with a vigor, and felicity and splendor of diction, greatly exceeding those of a premeditated speech, and that, too, in their own language, without a divine dictation of the words.

But the illustration chosen in support of verbal inspiration strikes me as far from satisfactory. Paul's speech before Agrippa is selected; and yet it is confessed that the entire speech is so natural to the man, that no one would think the speaker had divine aid at all, were it not for the promise of Jesus. Brother

McGarvey sees absolutely no reason for the Holy Spirit's aid, unless to guide in a selection of facts and in dictating the words in which these facts are presented. But neither in the selection of the facts, nor in the words which express them is there anything beyond the natural and acquired capacity of Paul. Why, then, intrude a power that is needless? Why make an outlay that is not required? Why insist on a miracle when no miracle is necessary? This is at war with the rigid economy of forces everywhere manifest in God's dealings with men. Christ's promise was to supply the apostles with divine aid in every emergency that required it. Beyond this there is no need to press the promise — though even if pressed here, it does not, as we have seen, involve a divine dictation of the words to be employed. To show how much of fancy enters into this illustration, let us turn to another instance in which Paul was brought before rulers (Acts xxiii). The high priest commanded that Paul should be smitten on the mouth. And Paul said unto him: " God shall smite thee, thou whited wall; and sittest thou to judge me according to the law, and commandest me to be smitten contrary to the law?" Will any one affirm that this outburst of indignation was dictated by the Spirit of God, and that the very words were God-breathed? What, then, will we make of what follows? "And they that stood by said, Revilest thou God's high priest? And Paul said, *I knew not*, brethren, that he was high priest; for it is written, Thou shalt not speak evil of a ruler of thy people." It is not our present province to inquire into the harmony of these facts with this or that theory of inspiration, but simply to show that the illustration of verbal inspiration based on them is inappropriate.

My good brother objects to the word *mechanical*, as applied to his theory; but what else than mechanical can we call that power which, on the day of Pentecost was manifest in the gift of tongues? The subjects of it used words of which they had no knowledge, no understanding. Their organs of speech were employed to utter they knew not what. There was no such free play and exaltation of their spiritual faculties as Brother McGarvey has described in Paul's case. It goes to show the failure of the effort to gather all the facts concerning inspiration within the embrace of the verbal or any other theory.

It is asked, since verbal inspiration is conceded in some cases, why not in all? It might as well be asked: Since in some cases inspired men were compelled to utter truth against their own will, why not in all cases? Since in some cases men uttered truths they did not understand, why not in all? If a direct answer to one interrogator is needed, we answer: because the facts in other cases do not warrant it. If asked how we are to decide in any case, as to the character or limits of the inspiration, we answer, by the attendant facts, circumstances, and declarations. If pressed with the question, how we are to attain to certainty in any given case, as to the teaching of any text, or on any subject, we answer, by the cumulative evidence of the passages in which the word in question, or the subject inquired about, appears. To suspend great conclusions on a single word in a single text, is not wise. The certainty we seek is found in the general tenor of Scripture teaching, which is not impaired by the uncertainty concerning any particular text.

The attempt to dispose of the difficulty suggested by Dean Alford concerning the different accounts of the inscription on the cross of Jesus is not successful. To say that there is an equal difficulty lying in the way of another theory is not satisfactory. We are not defending any particular theory. It must be shown that the facts in this case harmonize with the verbal inspiration theory. It has not been done. I think it cannot be done; I think, too, that the facts are reconcilable with another theory, but I am not called on here, in reply to my critics, to show this, nor have I the time for it.

The text in I. Cor. ii:13. I did not notice in the lectures, because I could not spare the space for a full exegesis, nor can I give it now the full consideration due to it. It is the strongest text the advocates of verbal inspiration have; and if it stood alone, it might perhaps be regarded as decisive proof of that view of inspiration. But, taken in connection with all else that is said on this subject, it must, I think, be otherwise interpreted than as teaching inspiration of the very words. "The words which man's wisdom teacheth" does not refer to the mere verbal utterance, but to the *thoughts* expressed and to the style of language as corresponding to those thoughts. It is not meant to say that the philosophers or rhetoricians referred to had a certain set of words in which they always expressed their thoughts; but that they taught certain things in a style of language adapted to their systems and born of their systems. In like manner the apostles preached certain great truths taught by the Spirit of God; and these truths they expressed, not in the language of the schools, but in the language adapted to, and, in fact, born of, the spiritual truths they uttered. Hence, although they might use many of the very words employed by the Grecian philosophers, they had a meaning, as employed in the Spirit's revelations, altogether different. As words of spiritual revelation, they carried a meaning and a fulness of power, unknown to them as words of philosophy or of Grecian rhetoric.

The theory of verbal inspiration does not account for many of the facts concerning inspiration in the Scriptures, which I have noted in the lectures. To say that the same is true of other theories, does not dispose of the difficulty. It only goes to show what was argued in the lectures — that while the *fact* of inspiration is clearly established, the *theories* of inspiration are all unsatisfactory.

Date

MICHIGAN
CHRISTIAN
COLLEGE
LIBRARY
ROCHESTER, MICH.